RUMSFELD

ReganBooks

An Imprint of HarperCollins*Publishers*

RUMSFELD

A PERSONAL PORTRAIT

MIDGE DECTER

All photographs courtesy of Joyce and Donald H. Rumsfeld
except for p. 146, David Kennerly; pp. 171 and 206, Robert D.
Ward; pp. 174, 190, and 194, Helene C. Stikkel.

HarperCollins books may be purchased for educational, business,
or sales promotional use. For information please write: Special Markets
Department, HarperCollins Publishers Inc., 10 East 53rd Street,
New York, NY 10022.

FIRST EDITION

Designed by Judith Stagnitto Abbate/Abbate Design

Printed on acid-free paper

Library of Congress Cataloging-in-Publication Data
Decter, Midge.
    Rumsfeld : a personal portrait / Midge Decter.—1st ed.
    p. cm.
    ISBN 0-06-056091-6 (acid-free paper)
    1. Rumsfeld, Donald, 1932– 2. Cabinet officers—United States—
Biography. 3. United States. Dept. of Defense—Officials and
employees—Biography. 4. War on Terrorism, 2001– I. Title.
E840.8.R84D43 2003
355'.0092—dc22
[B]
2003058558

03 04 05 06 07 BVG/RRD 10 9 8 7 6 5 4 3 2 1

For Arnold Beichman, another of life's warriors,
and a lesson to us all

CONTENTS

ACKNOWLEDGMENTS

M ANY PEOPLE were most generous to me, taking time out of their busy lives to answer what I fear might have seemed to them my tiresome questions. For that and other kindnesses I wish to thank Kenneth and Carol Adelman, James Denny, Steven Herbitz, Martin Hoffman, Muggy Hoffman, Debby Jannotta, Ned Jannotta, Nick Marshall, Richard Perle, Margaret Robson, James Schlesinger, and Paul Wolfowitz. Andrew Marshall graciously and patiently tried to relieve my ignorance. Even more special thanks are owed to the members of the Rumsfeld family: Don's sister, Joan Ramsay, and her husband, Alan Ramsay; the Rumsfeld children, Marcy and Nick Rumsfeld and Valerie Richard; and last but very far from least, Joyce Rumsfeld, who found time for me in the course of what had to have been a pressing, crowded, and worrisome period, a period, moreover, saddened by the death of her mother in the winter of 2003. And, of course, the secretary himself, who in the midst of looking after two wars not only found time for me but caused myriad valuable documents to be placed in my hands. Which brings me to Colonel George Rhynedance, a gentleman who, with many other things to do, was at no end of bother to answer my requests for material, which he did with the kind of promptness and good cheer that I can only hope to emulate some day.

Last in the list, but far from least, are two people without whom even the first word of this project could most likely not have been set down on paper. They were thoughtful, endlessly helpful from day one to the end, and as they both know, my getting to know them was among the best of all the many pleasures connected with this book: Arlene Nestel and Nancy Pardo. That Rumsfeld found them both and chose them to assist him—Nancy Pardo in Chicago and Arlene Nestel in the Pentagon—is about as good a tribute to the soundness of his judgment as any I can think of.

I also want to thank my agent, Lynn Chu, who is a friend as well as an unfailingly dependable adviser; Monica Crowley, who offered me so much encouragement; and Cassie Jones, who has for the second time made the editorial process something to look forward to.

RUMSFELD

PRELUDE

I T WAS a warm autumn evening in 2001, and we were dining alfresco on a terrace overlooking New York's Central Park. A woman I had known for many years—a handsome, elegant, and well-connected member of the city's cultural and artistic community—was seated across from me, and as dinner wore on, the name of Donald Rumsfeld came up in the conversation. As it would, from then on, so many times.

"Oh, *Rumsfeld*," she practically cooed, "I just *love* the man! To tell you the truth, I have his picture hanging in my dressing room."

I was startled. In what was clearly a most interesting life, this very clever woman had known many famous and important men, and the idea that so cool and worldly a denizen of New York society had hung Donald Rumsfeld's picture in her dressing room as a smitten girl might do (assuming that a smitten girl even had a dressing room) left me in a state of wonderment. What was going on here?

I myself had known Rumsfeld for a number of years, though I cannot say I had known him well. Our connection had been largely professional, in that years earlier I had been the director of an organization for which he had served as honorary chairman. What I had mainly known of him, then, was that he was someone immensely intelligent and tough-minded, and an untiring advocate of a strong American defense. I had been very pleased then, as one would be in the case of someone one knows and respects, when after more than a quarter of a century he had been returned to a high position in the United States government. But for him to be the object of so very feminine a kind of admiration was something altogether different. This was the stuff—no other word would do—of glamour.

In the days and weeks that followed, I would encounter a number of other women who made roughly the same kind of response to the mention of the name Rumsfeld. Moreover, unlike my dinner companion, some of these women were, to put it mildly, inclined to be far from sympathetic to his political orientation and that of the administration he had been appointed to serve.

Nor, to be sure, was this "discovery" of Rumsfeld a topic of conversation for women only. Men too—including men who had likely known nothing of him before—seemed to be paying special attention and speaking of him in tones of the highest admiration.

He was at that point still the country's relatively new secretary of defense and thus, one might have thought, hardly a figure to have attracted either that particular kind or amount of public notice. True, the country had just gone through the trauma of discovering on 9/11 that America, too, was vulnerable to terrorist attack. We were now at war in Afghanistan. And true, the secretary of defense was someone with a major part of the responsibility for overseeing the direction of that war. Still, there was a quality to the attention being paid him that went beyond both his title and his role. Indeed, with only a few exceptions it is to be doubted whether many people—except, of course, for those with a specially keen interest in the affairs of government—can remember either the names or years of service of all but a few of their country's past secretaries of defense.

Moreover, in a long and very far from undistinguished career Rumsfeld had also been a congressman, director of a government agency, a diplomat, a White House chief of staff, a successful businessman, and he had even, albeit briefly, run for president—all without his virtues and attractions having become the subject of heated conversation at fashionable New York dinner parties. Yet here now was Donald Rumsfeld, whose name and fame were being sung all over town.

In time, of course, there would be another war, and with it even greater admiration for the man in charge. Along with much controversy, particularly among America's allies (or perhaps the more accurate term will have turned out to be America's former allies) in Western Europe.

Just how all this had come to pass and what it might mean were, I thought, questions that merited some serious looking into.

And thus the story that follows—told, as it were, in mid-flight.

INTRODUCTION

O N DECEMBER 13, 2000, possibly the most agonizing presidential election in the country's history finally came to an end with the decision by the Supreme Court that George W. Bush was to be the forty-third president of the United States. The thirty-six days it took to arrive at this decision had, to put it mildly, been nerve-racking for everyone concerned: for Bush himself, for his Democratic opponent Al Gore, for their respective parties, and most emphatically for the country's voters. (Even some Democrats may have been heard to sigh with relief that, losers though they were, at least the long suspense was over.)

But if there was relief, there was a great deal of bitterness, too. Legitimately or not, the Democrats felt that the election had been stolen from them. Certain Republicans were also less than jubilant, worried that by putting the outcome of the contest into the hands of the Supreme Court, the leaders of their party had set a precedent that might one day come back to bite them. Even the president-elect himself may have had a few bad moments. For the voters had split the country virtually evenly between its two Democratic coasts and that great Republican swath that extends across the rest. The map that illustrated this pattern by means of the colors red and blue was broadcast over and over in the days following the election, and George W. Bush himself might have felt at least a few tremors of disquiet if and when he happened to see it. Being president of the United States is a plum that many men have coveted and striven to possess, but to govern the country that had given him so vividly divided a mandate would be no easy matter. That map was nothing so much as a visual promise of stormy days ahead.

Now, in addition to being the seat of the federal government, Washington, D.C., is home to an inveterate band of politics-and-government addicts. These are the people, both in and out of government, in whose lives post-election days are normally a time for the high entertainment of predicting and/or passing knowing judgment on presidential appointments. This time, however, their fun had not only been foreshortened but seemed to have lost some of its normal bettors' good humor. For the often highly entertaining period of exchanging phone calls, extracting favors, and circulating resumés known as "the transition" had been most unentertainingly abbreviated.

So it was that not until December 28 did the new president-elect announce his choice for the job of secretary of defense: Donald H. Rumsfeld. Rumor had it that Rumsfeld was actually Bush's second choice to become what is known in Washington bureaucratese as "SecDef." According to the *Washington Post*, Bush had first discussed the appointment with former Indiana Senator Dan Coats, who seems to have lost out, or so gossip had it, by asking for reassurance that he would not have to be subordinate to Colin Powell, the popular incoming secretary of state. Be that as it may, Rumsfeld was both a longtime good friend and former mentor of Vice President–elect Richard Cheney, and Cheney had no doubt reassured Bush that Rumsfeld would neither ask for nor need any such promise—that he could, in other words, most skillfully take care of himself.

The new nominee was not only someone who had served long years in Washington as a three-plus-terms congressman from Illinois, a White House official for both Richard Nixon and Gerald Ford, and a diplomat, he had even for a brief time in the mid-seventies served as President Gerald Ford's secretary of defense. In addition, after the inauguration of Jimmy Carter, when the Ford administration decamped and Rumsfeld left Washington to move back to his native Illinois, he had been called upon more than once to fulfill some presidential or congressional mission.

Thus the betting line among the Washington insiders was that Rumsfeld's appointment was on the whole not only sound but shrewd. He had spent his time out of Washington as a businessman and had earned himself a reputation in the nation's business community as a highly successful manager—and manage, after all, is what the secretary of defense primarily does. In recent years, he had also made a name for himself as an expert on a number of urgent issues of national defense—a subject that had been of the keenest interest to him even before his first stint at the Pentagon. Moreover, so far as anyone could remember he had ended his rather brief tour as head of the Department of Defense on cordial terms with the military.

On the other hand, among some of the *really* knowing, Rumsfeld's having been named to any cabinet post at all had come as something of a surprise. For it was no secret to such as they that the President-elect's father—George H. W. Bush, the forty-first President—had once harbored rather less than kindly feelings toward his son's new appointee. This problem dated from as long

ago as the days when the two men were together in the Ford administration. For that was the time when Bush *père,* then the
American ambassador to China, had been brought back to Washington from Beijing in order to become the director of Central
Intelligence. Bush mistakenly believed that becoming head of the
CIA would forever ruin his chance at the presidency. Rumsfeld
was at that point serving as Ford's chief of staff, and Bush had held
him responsible for what he regarded as a plot to put him out to
pasture. Now whether the father had softened after so many years
or the son had simply decided to pay no attention to the problem,
if indeed it was a problem, even the insiders who counted themselves the farthest "inside" were no longer prepared to say with any
certainty. But for a time at least they would be watching with the
most careful attention for any gossip-worthy signs of strain in
precincts close to the presidency.

R UMSFELD WAS sworn into office during the morning of
January 26, 2001, and later that afternoon he was greeted outside the Pentagon with the kind of celebratory welcome that the
military accords to each new secretary of defense: namely, a military parade replete with fifes and drums, an honor guard, a big
brass band, and soldiers, sailors, marines, members of the air force,
and coastguardsmen marching behind and beneath a veritable
symphony of regimental and state flags. To the younger members
of the military brass who were making his acquaintance for the first
time, the secretary might have appeared to be somewhat dwarfed
by the pomp of the occasion. He was not tall, nor particularly
broad, nor did he carry himself in the manner of someone well-
acquainted with wielding authority. In fact, his many years as a man
of some consequence had not had the slightest effect on his bear-

ing, which gave no sign of his ever having become conscious of, let alone concerned with, any of the outward marks of his success and/or importance. Standing next to the militarily erect chairman of the Joint Chiefs of Staff, General Henry Shelton, he seemed not quite to fill out his overcoat, and when the two men walked side by side out on the field in order to review the troops, Rumsfeld appeared, especially by comparison with his companion, to cut an unceremonious and rather shambling figure.

Later there was a reception in one of the corridors of the Pentagon. As the new secretary and his wife, Joyce, stood together greeting and receiving congratulations from those who had gathered for the occasion, she was heard to remark to an acquaintance who had stopped to shake her hand, "Can you *believe* it? I woke up this morning and said, 'We are here *again*.'"

Here they were again, after twenty-four years, and on that afternoon as they stood watching the parade outside the Pentagon, the terrain must have seemed familiar. But what would happen to them before the year 2001 was out no one, certainly not they, could have even begun to imagine. Rumsfeld would find himself embroiled in conflict within his department, particularly with the army; the World Trade Center and the Pentagon would be deliberately hit by three hijacked commercial airliners; the country would go to war in—of all places—Afghanistan, and not long after that in Iraq; and after nearly forty years in and out of public life the secretary would become known to millions as "Rummy," America's newest television star.

A STAR IS BORN

DONALD RUMSFELD is a Chicagoan. His life has carried him to many places, primary among them, of course, Washington. Nor, though he was born in Chicago on July 9, 1932, did he grow up there, but rather in Winnetka, one of the suburbs located north of the city along the shore of Lake Michigan. Moreover, by the time he left for Washington to serve in the Bush cabinet he had been living within Chicago proper for only sixteen years. Nevertheless, a child of that great, energetic, hard-driving, open-faced, middle western American city is what Rumsfeld most recognizably is.

"One of the two shaping experiences of my life," he says, "was

The second time around: George W. Bush and his new/old Secretary of Defense

the Depression. I still stop to pick up a penny. The other, of course, was World War II."

On the day he was born the average annual income in the United States was $1,652. A pound of butter cost 28 cents, a gallon of gas cost a dime, and the average price of a new home was $6,500. Herbert Hoover was in the White House but would not be there for long: Earlier in that same week the Democratic party had nominated a New Yorker named Franklin D. Roosevelt to be its candidate for president. As for Chicago, now a lively center of finance and commerce, it was at that moment the city best known in American legend for the crime in its streets, crime that would for the most part be stilled after 1933 by the repeal of the Eighteenth Amendment and the end of Prohibition. It was also the city that had not that many years earlier been eulogized by Carl Sandburg, its informally recognized poet laureate, as the "hog-butcher for the world."

When their son Donald was two and their daughter Joan four and a half, George and Jeanette Rumsfeld moved the family northward, first briefly to Evanston and then a bit farther on to Winnetka. (Indeed, *briefly* is a word that would continue to apply, by most people's standards rather dramatically, to virtually all Rumsfeld domiciles, whether those of Don's parents or later those in which he himself was to live as an adult. For by his own not necessarily complete listing of them, he has in the course of his life so far had some thirty-four different addresses in more than twenty different towns and cities.)

George Rumsfeld, the infant Don's father, had been working for Baird and Warner, a real-estate firm operating in the region. He had worked his way up from office boy to agent, and he calculated that the places where real-estate values would be both highest and most stable were communities whose populations were most committed to the idea of providing their children with a superior education.

George Rumsfeld's perception would turn out not only to be sound but positively fateful—the word does not seem too strong—as far as his children were concerned. For as it would turn out, by 1964 the Illinois 13th Congressional District, for a long time made up completely of Chicago's northern lakeside suburbs, would vie with only two other districts in the United States (one in California and one in Virginia) for having the highest median level of education (12.6 years). And this, in turn, suggests that the residents of those suburbs had for some time also been enjoying an unusually high degree of affluence—wealth, after all, being a significant factor in the rate of high school graduation and college attendance. Indeed, in that same census the Illinois 13th was found to be first in the nation for having both the highest median income and the lowest rate of unemployment. Thus the move northward, where—though the Depression would for some time continue to mean that even in the northern suburbs there would be a number of people struggling to make a living—prospects for the future were nevertheless brighter.

So the idea about where the Rumsfelds should live after Chicago had been borne out, and then some. To visit Wilmette, Winnetka, Evanston, et al., today is to be offered visible confirmation of how long-standing and deeply rooted their present-day affluence has proved to be. The area boasts street after street of large, handsome, unself-consciously costly houses built in an older, non-chic, more settled and stable, more self-confident, middle-western style than is nowadays so frequently to be found in the suburbs of the well-to-do.

The Rumsfelds, however, were not fated to join in Winnetka's inevitable affluence. Their own income would prove at best to be modest and hard-earned. Moreover, when the United States went to war against Germany and Japan—Don now nine and a half and Joan going on twelve—George decided that he had to serve in the military and opted to volunteer for the navy: whatever else you can say about it, not, to put it mildly, a move likely to result in any enhancement of the family coffers.

As it happened, George Rumsfeld was a slight man and extremely thin. In addition, he was quite a bit older than the recruits then being taken into service. Thus when he first volunteered, the navy turned him down. But he was determined to take part in the war and spent the year trying to build himself up, copiously drinking milk shakes, his son says, and eating bananas. (Determination

may not be a heritable trait, but to judge from George's son, it was surely one on marked display during young Rumsfeld's formative years.) Meanwhile, the war was going badly, and in 1942 the armed forces decided that they were going to have to expand the pool of potential manpower and upped the age of eligibility for recruitment. So it was that in 1943 the navy relented toward George Rumsfeld and inducted him. He had by then passed his thirty-eighth birthday.

Now, anyone who was growing up in those years would undoubtedly endorse Donald Rumsfeld's view that World War II had been a, probably *the,* formative experience of his life. For coming out of the Depression doldrums, the United States was being mobilized. It was being mobilized in a whole variety of ways, morally and spiritually as well as militarily. To have been a child in those years was to have all of a boy's most innocent, high-hearted childhood convictions about what was good and bad, heroic and cowardly—in short, what was to be done and what not done, honored and not honored—confirmed by the entire world around one. And in Donald Rumsfeld's case in particular, this experience would if anything be intensified by the life around his own military-centered family hearth.

Or rather, hearths. Though this fact about her seemed, at least in later years, to have been largely hidden from the wider public view, Jeanette Rumsfeld was a woman whose own determination must easily have been a match for her husband's. For when George Rumsfeld was accepted by the navy, she made up her mind that she and the children would follow him wherever his being in the service happened to take them.

New Trier Muscle

It would in fact take them, first, to a somewhat downtrodden district of Elizabeth City, North Carolina, from there to temporary navy housing in East Port Orchard, Washington, and from there, finally, to Coronado, California. In North Carolina, Jeanette realized that if she were to follow her plan, she would have to learn to drive, and so she did, although to begin with somewhat timorously. In East Port Orchard, on discovering that her husband was being assigned to a carrier berthed in Southern California and still a neophyte behind the wheel, she set out in the car she had not yet fully mastered and moved herself and the children down the West Coast to Coronado. (And thereby hangs a family legend. On this trip they would go through San Francisco, a city world-famous for the cinematic steepness of its hills. Jeanette would make Don and Joan get out of the car each time she had to navigate a seriously hilly patch. They would walk and she would drive along beside them until she found herself again on level ground and could allow them back into the car.)

Years later, a friend and fellow high school student named Nick Marshall would remember once remarking to Don that Jeanette Rumsfeld seemed to him to have been "a forties character, like June Allyson," the actress who in a number of World War II films wept copiously across the movie screens of America. "Oh, no," demurred Jeanette's son. "My mother was a *strong* woman."[1]

---

[1] Which was something Marshall himself might have imagined, since by his own account, while he himself had been a more or less typical teenage slob, Don Rumsfeld was quite the opposite, "always," as Marshall put it, "so darn clean," never to be seen without a sparkling white T-shirt and neatly ironed khaki pants. If this said something about the boy himself, it surely said more about the determination of his mother.

"You've got to be a football hero. . . ."

In 1945 with the war now over, the Rumsfeld family returned to Illinois, this time—though again briefly—to another of the northern suburbs of Chicago, Glencoe. They had been away for roughly three years. Now, three years is not a lifetime, not even in a time of war, and not even for a boy going on ten. Still, his mother's having determined that she and her children would not remain behind in leafy suburban comfort but would instead live in whatever places and under whatever conditions the war service of their father happened to dictate was bound to leave its mark on him. If nothing else, it must have been a hopeful early lesson in how to live and thrive in a life of changing venues and circumstances.

Years afterward, Don would engage Margaret Robson, the wife of another lifelong friend, John Robson—a woman whose early life in a small town in Minnesota had been constantly shadowed by the threat of serious poverty—in a running jocular argument about which of them had had to hold more after-school and summer jobs. And each time they argued, she said, the number of jobs he would claim to have been saddled with—newsboy, magazine salesman, gardener, part-time mailman, etc.—would grow. But though the Rumsfelds were far from rich, it does not seem to be the case, at least once George was out of the navy, that they lived under or even near the shadow of what could be called genuine poverty. For one thing, the country was rapidly moving into better times. For another, George was not only a strong-willed but an enterprising man. He would, for example, move the family into a house that was in a condition so bad he could buy it for a song, fix it up, sell it, and move on to the next one. (Later he would keep them and put them up for rent.) Rumsfeld remembers that the family had lived in three different houses on the same street. He also remembers coming home from school on many an afternoon and helping to scrape old wallpaper off the walls. His mother, who worked as a substitute schoolteacher, would also come home from school each day and join in the labor.

This was perhaps not the easiest way to make a living in the real-estate business, but it was also not in the running for being desperately poor. For one thing, it was in its way far too enterprising to permit any feelings of discouragement. Chances are, then, that at least some of Don's after-school earnings were the result not so much of brute necessity as of pride in carrying his weight.

For instance, while the family was living in North Carolina, each day an old black man with a horse and wagon would come by their street selling watermelons. In a feeble voice and indecipherable accent the old man would call out something unintelligible and move on. Not surprisingly, he had very few customers. Don had been observing the old man's difficulties, and one day he approached him with a proposition: He would help sell the watermelons if for every ten he sold, he would be given one free. What the old man thought of either the cheek or the cleverness of the boy was never discovered, but the deal was struck. Whereupon the new salesman, who climbed down from the wagon and approached potential customers—calling out his wares in a way that could be heard and understood, began to rack up a notable increase in sales for the old man and at the same time brought home a number of watermelons that he was then able to sell on his own account. The proceeds could not have been great, surely not enough to make much difference to the family exchequer. But his belief in the efficacy of enterprise must have received a firm implantation.

Another job, one that would have a decisive effect on the course of his later life, was that of counselor at a ranch called the Philmont Ranch, which was run by the Boy Scouts in New Mexico. Don joined the Boy Scouts and became, in keeping with the determination he would show throughout the rest of his life, an Eagle Scout. He was chosen from far-off Illinois to work at the ranch during the summer. Among other things he rode on horse-back through some of that state's magnificent high desert and fell in love with the place. (He never forgot it. Many years later, in 1982, he would buy some property there and to this day escapes to his farm in Taos whenever he has the opportunity.)

In 1946, a year after the family's return to Illinois, Don entered New Trier High School. Located in Winnetka and serving several of the surrounding communities, New Trier continues to be notable for being one of those high-achieving suburban American high schools—some would say the highest achieving in the nation—whose graduates have famously gone on to distinguish themselves in a wide variety of fields: law, business, politics, journalism, and the arts and entertainment (it was, for example, the high school attended by such famous stars of the silver screen as Ralph Bellamy, Charlton Heston, Ann-Margret, Rock Hudson, Bruce Dern, and Hugh O'Brien). Serving a group of increasingly affluent communities, New Trier has down through the years been able to offer even more in the way of programs and facilities than most other schools of its kind. Founded in 1901, by 1990 it boasted among other things its own TV studios and some twenty-six different interscholastic sports. Moreover, though the process by which educational traditions get established remains something of a mystery, the glow that is associated with the name "New Trier" may by itself have had something to do with the institution's role in the lives of its graduates. For all over the country there are people who, no matter how old or how accomplished, continue to identify themselves with the school and with the time they spent and the friends they made there.

In any case, whether this was peculiarly characteristic of the school itself or of the makeup of its student body—or of Donald Rumsfeld's own makeup—New Trier would continue to be a powerful presence in his life. A goodly number of the friendships he would make there would persist and remain strong and influential through all the circumstances of a highly various life. (One weekend in May 2003, for instance, with the war in Iraq essentially wound down to a policing mission, Don and Joyce would entertain thirty couples, friends from their New Trier days and spouses, with whom they continue to keep in touch.)

In high school he worked and played hard and was an all-around citizen. He went out for football (though he was too small and too light make the varsity team), swam, played a little basketball, and did some running. But his main athletic passion—in high school, in college, and later in the United States navy—was as a wrestler. Now, wrestling is a somewhat uncommon and in its way a rather solitary sport. One must, for instance, basically train oneself to be a wrestler, particularly the kind of championship wrestler that Don Rumsfeld turned out to be, without the support and camaraderie that are so central to the games played by teams. Moreover, training oneself to be a wrestler is a particularly grueling process. According to Ned Jannotta, a fellow New Trier graduate, Chicago banker, and lifelong friend, a clear connection can be traced between Rumsfeld's experience as a wrestler and certain of his most outstanding traits of character. "Wrestling," says Jannotta, "is after all a sport in which there is no such thing as second-place money. You go head to head, winner take all." And as a high-school wrestler Don would take much, winning award after award.

New Trier was also the place where he met and took a greater and greater interest in a classmate named Joyce Pierson, who would one day be his wife. Like Don, Joyce too had had something of a peripatetic childhood. Her father, Red Pierson, had been a salesman and then sales manager for the International Harvester Company, and his job had carried the family from Billings,

Montana, where Joyce was born, to Fargo, North Dakota, to Minneapolis, Minnesota, to Milwaukee, Wisconsin, and finally, to Chicago and a home in Wilmette.

Joyce's mother, Marion, had been born in a small town in western Minnesota and had grown up in Montana, but exactly how or why her family had made the move west seems by now to have been lost in the mists of memory. Though this happened in the twentieth century, it does not seem altogether far-fetched to imagine—or anyway, as Joyce's future life as the wife of Donald Rumsfeld offers a tantalizing suggestion—that at some point one of those unbelievably brave women who trekked westward in their Conestoga wagons, enduring God alone knows what hardships and bringing with them the makings of civilization, set herself down in the western wilderness and produced the daughter who eventually produced Joyce.

At New Trier, while Don was an athlete as well as a general contributor to the civic life of the school, Joyce, while also active in student affairs, tended to focus on things more artistic. By the time of their graduation, the couple must both have seemed, and seemed not, to have what used in old-fashioned parlance to be called "an understanding." Don was given a scholarship to Princeton, while Joyce decided that she wanted to go in the opposite direction—that is, to the University of Colorado in Boulder. Her explanation for choosing Boulder is that had she gone to school somewhere in the East, she would have been too distracted as she sat around waiting for Don to call when she knew full well that he wouldn't do so. (Since Princeton was then an all-male school, any girl a young man wanted to see had to be imported and put up there, and Don had no money to spend on such a project.

The wrestler

According to him, he had no more than two or three dates during the whole four years he spent there.) So she chose instead to use her time in college studying, getting herself an education in art history, and refusing, as it were, to sit by the phone waiting for him to call. This decision on her part may have been the result of a sturdy, sensible, and serious ambition. Perhaps, too, it had also been something of a strategy. Where affairs of the heart are concerned, who

can really say? In any case, she studied seriously, and if her decision had had anything to do with strategy, conscious or unconscious, it turned out in the end to have been a wise, not to say a fateful, one.

Don entered Princeton in 1950, and speaking of fateful, he opted to concentrate on government and politics. He also corresponded with Joyce off in Colorado and would from time to time keep her abreast of what was clearly becoming a major passion of his life by recommending books about government and politics for her to read. (He did visit her there as well, and, as she describes it, learned to ski in one fell and speedy swoop.[2]) He also continued to wrestle and win trophy after trophy. He engaged, too, in a sideline of betting on his capacity to perform one-handed push-ups in order to earn himself some badly needed pocket money.

In his sophomore year, he was selected in a national competition for a naval ROTC scholarship, which meant that after graduating he would follow the family tradition and join the navy for a minimum of three years (though in his case as an officer). As it would turn out, he would serve not, like his father, on a carrier but in the naval air force, where he would train in formation flying and where he would become a flight instructor and ultimately an instructor of flight instructors. He would also, by the way, win the All Navy Wrestling Championship.

Through the Princeton years Joyce clearly continued to be a serious, even if for long stretches physically far-off, presence in his life. After graduation in the spring of 1954, on his very first morn-

---

[2] Many years later, Rumsfeld's son Nicholas would say of his father that he "doesn't ski as if he's *on* a mountain, he skis as if he wants to *move* it."

Joyce Pierson, graduate

ing home, he interrupted his breakfast, went over to Joyce's house, and asked her to marry him. Then, so legend has it, as soon as she said yes, he returned home where a college friend was awaiting him for lunch. "Not very classy," he laughs.

They were married on December 27, 1954, and took off for the Naval Air Station in Pensacola, Florida. In Florida Don learned to fly while Joyce commenced to sustain the Rumsfeld-Pierson tradition of setting up and taking down households and living arrangements and quickly moving on to new ones. (After only twelve and a half years of marriage, they were to have moved more than ten times.) From Pensacola, they were sent first to Corpus Christi, Texas, then to Norfolk, Virginia, and then back to Pensacola. For him his time in the naval air force—and the experience of training others—would be his first adult taste of the energizing effect, as well as the burden, of leadership. For her it would be a proving ground for polishing the high (and largely lost) art of making oneself and those around one comfortable under a variety of less than normally convenient circumstances. "She was a trouper," her husband remarks. "Many times I had to be off somewhere, and she would make the move, and set up the house, all by herself."

In Pensacola the Rumsfelds were to cross paths with their old New Trier—and Princeton—friend Ned Jannotta, who had also joined the navy and become a pilot. Finding themselves together at that time and in that place may have seemed to them something of a coincidence, but on the other hand, it could just as easily have seemed like a perfectly natural state of affairs. For serving in the armed forces was viewed as a more or less inevitable next step in the lives of a large number of Don's classmates, and indeed of his

The wedding, December 27, 1954

contemporaries generally. The Korean War had only recently come to an end, the Cold War was now in full flood, and the draft, albeit more relaxed than in the wartime years, remained in force. Above all, the idea of service to the nation still weighed heavily in many a young man's sense of duty, both to himself and to his country.

It would take more than another decade for such an idea to be spoken of first with irony and then with scorn. Meanwhile, the world was and would remain a dangerous place, and for a great number of young men—if not, indeed, for a whole generation of them—the United States was its best hope.

On duty to self and country

2

MR. RUMSFELD GOES
TO WASHINGTON

WHETHER THE idea of a career somewhere in the
public service had been in his mind since childhood or whether, as he himself has sometimes
claimed, the ambition had been fixed there by his
studies at Princeton, it somehow seems natural that on leaving the
navy Rumsfeld would next move in on Washington, D.C.

John Keegan, the distinguished military historian, published a
profile of him in the February 2003 issue of *Vanity Fair.* Keegan
opened the piece with the observation that Rumsfeld's having been
a Princeton man might help explain his being "man of the hour" as
secretary of defense. For, said Keegan, Princeton is the most mili-

A would-be congressman and a former president

tary of the Ivy League colleges: the school to which, before the Civil War, rich Southerners sent their sons and from which, before 1917, young Americans volunteered to fight in the Great War. Princetonians, Keegan continued, "are not too proud to fight at all. They do their duty as if it comes naturally." (Whether Princeton continues to be the school Keegan remembers is a question, but for Don and many of his friends and classmates there was no doubt that going into the service was something they had indeed come to take for granted.)

Washington had probably been not only a natural but an inevitable next move. He clearly did not care about making money—and would have none to speak of for years to come. Where, then, would a fiercely energetic and ambitious young man interested in public service be likely to go if not to the nation's capital?

From 1957 through most of 1960, he would be learning his way around Capitol Hill, in particular the House of Representatives. He first found a job in the office of Representative David Dennison of Ohio, working as the congressman's administrative assistant. He also served for a while as staff assistant to Representative Robert Griffin of Michigan, following which he briefly moved back among the Ohioans in order to manage David Dennison's campaign for reelection. (Unfortunately, the candidate was defeated, but the campaign manager learned a great deal that would very soon be useful to him.) During this period he also spent some time attending classes at Georgetown Law School, though it soon became clear that the law was not to be any part of his own future.

By now the Rumsfelds had two daughters, Valerie, born in 1956, and Marcy, born in 1960. In this period of Don's introduction to the finer arts of politics and politicians, Joyce, for her part, now had two little ones for whom to provide the maximum degree of comfort and amenity on a minimum amount both of cash and permanence. That is to say, from 1958 to late 1960 the Rumsfelds were to move five more times—and finally a sixth, as Don, clearly having turned his mind to the prospect of a political career of his own, would return to Illinois and wait for a chance to get into the game.

As it happened, this would not take him long. For a brief time he would attempt to stay afloat by serving as a "registered representative" of A. G. Becker and Company, Chicago investment bankers. Which seems to have meant, in simple English, that he became a bond salesman. This could hardly have been a congenial occupation for a young man restless to be on his way into public life. But like the watermelons of yore, he no doubt attacked the job full bore while he was at it.

Then, in late November of 1961, the opening he was waiting for arrived. Congresswoman Marguerite Stitt Church, a Republican who had been representing the 13th District for some sixteen years, announced that she would not be running for reelection. A primary to select a Republican candidate to replace her was to be held on the following April 10, and Don decided that here was his chance to get into the game.

He was young, not yet thirty, and both poor and without any impressive source of either financial or political backing—except, to begin with, for a group of his and Joyce's old friends and schoolmates from New Trier. The first meeting of the Rumsfeld campaign committee, then, was a gathering of a handful of people, among them Ned Jannotta, who had agreed to become campaign manager, and John Robson, a relatively new graduate of the Harvard Law School who would appear again and again at critical junctures in Don's career and would for now be the campaign's issues director. As Jannotta remembers it, when the meeting was about to break up, someone in the room suddenly said, "By the way, won't we be needing some money?" Whereupon those assembled managed to pony up the munificent sum of $375, and yet another old friend, a fellow wrestler and Princeton alumnus named Brad Glass, was appointed campaign treasurer. An old house belonging to George Rumsfeld that happened to be standing empty would serve as campaign headquarters.

Despite this unpromising start, by April of 1962 Don had managed to attract something like 1,500 volunteers, most of them very young, very active, and very determined—especially, it seems, the young women among them. "The women," Jannotta remembers, "basically did all the work." Except, Jannotta adds, "for the candidate himself, who will still, as he did then, outwork anybody," and who during the campaign was, among other things, out shaking hands at some train station or other in the district every morning from 6:00 A.M. on. By April, too, George Rumsfeld's fellow realtors were grumbling that all over the district, virtually wherever one looked, Rumsfeld campaign signs had been pounded into front lawns.

Indefatigable as the candidate may have been, however (and difficult as it is now to believe), the Rumsfeld campaign had at first suffered from the fact that the candidate was not an effective speaker. Whereupon he found himself a speech coach and practiced assiduously. Once or twice he even hired a meeting hall and invited about a dozen or so of his friends to come and listen to him and offer their criticisms. Which they proceeded to do, without showing any particular tenderness for his feelings. Once again, the same determination that had earlier produced those wrestling championships would prove invaluable. For by the end of the cam-

Congressman-to-be, with daughter Marcy

paign, Rumsfeld had managed to become his own most effective spokesman.

Between the time he decided to run, in December 1961, and the primary in April 1962, the field of Republican would-be candidates was narrowed, first from six to four, and finally from four to two. Throughout the campaign his opponents had been making an

issue of Rumsfeld's age and inexperience, but over the course of the winter a number of the leading businessmen in the district had been persuaded to back him, which played an important role in laying that particular issue to rest. So, too, it seems, with most if not all of the other issues raised against him. For he won the primary handily, and on April 11, the *Chicago Daily News* carried the headline—which could from the perspective of forty years later be called the prophecy—"Rumsfeld: New Star for GOP."

The following November the "new star" was elected, as they say, in a walk. As he would also be in the three congressional elections that followed.

The life of a congressman's family, for Joyce as well as for Don, would prove to have its deep satisfactions—along with what less energetic or resourceful people might have found its nearly insuperable difficulties. The Rumsfelds believed, for example, that a Congressman ought actually to live in his district at least some part of the year. Thus, until the practice began to make too much difficulty for their daughter Valerie in school—the District of Columbia and Chicago suburban schools proving to be rather seriously out of sync—they set out to spend half the year in Washington and the other half in Glenview, Illinois. This entailed repeatedly packing the household into the back of the family station wagon—two little girls (one of them hardly more than a baby), clothes, needed household goods, food, cats, kittens—finding a tenant to occupy and help defray the expenses of the house that would now be empty, and trekking somewhat less than halfway across the country either in an eastward or westward direction.

Once the Rumsfeld daughters, Marcy age three or four and

"Vote Rumsfeld"—the 13th District would do so four times.

Valerie age seven or eight, were interviewed by a Chicago paper and asked how they felt about living in two places. "I like my friends in Illinois better than my friends in Washington," Valerie confessed. "You get to sleep on things," said Marcy. Intrigued by the innocent profundity of this remark, the interviewer wished for Marcy to say a little more on the matter, until it was explained that the child's answer had been literal: As they traveled back and forth, Marcy would spend a good deal of time sleeping on the "things" piled up in the back of the wagon.

That such an arrangement could not go on for too long was predictable, but that it should have been tried at all was surely the mark of deep commitment to the principle of mind over matter. In any case, had they persisted, the birth of Nicholas Rumsfeld in June 1967 would surely have required an end to the caravanning.

Not that the voters in the 13th District would have been likely to demand, or even expect, that their representative impose such hardship on himself and his family: The annual trek, in other words, had surely sprung from some exclusively Rumsfeldian idea about the duties of representation. For he quite regularly conducted polls among his constituents, and from the earliest poll on it was clear (as, of course, he already knew) that the district's voters were on the whole a conservative and generally unruffled lot: Nearly 60 percent favored a balanced budget, some 80 percent were for cuts in foreign aid, and roughly 75 percent for sanctions on Cuba. Not the kind of people to think of overburdening the wife and children of their congressman—or the congressman himself, for that matter.

A new congressional family: Don, Valerie, Marcy, and Joyce

S OON AFTER his arrival in Congress, Rumsfeld began to attract what, especially for a freshman, was a goodly amount of attention. In July 1963, for instance, along with five colleagues, he would issue a complaint that by concentrating NASA so exclusively on the possibility of going to the moon, the government was ignoring "the main thrust of the Soviet space aim, which is to dominate inner space (100 to 500 miles) . . . ."[1] In only six months, remarked the *Chicago Tribune,* Rumsfeld had "become an expert in a field where there were few rivals." During that same month, he also criticized the State Department for the way it had recently been engaging in friendly relations with the Soviet Union's Nikita Khrushchev and Hungary's János Kádár.

Later in the year he emerged as a vocal (and unsuccessful) opponent of cutting taxes without making any compensatory spending cuts, calling it "government by IOU." He also got involved in a controversy over a civil rights bill. While he favored the bill in principle, he opposed certain of its provisions that he believed were unconstitutional. He therefore supported a substitute bill and stood his ground under a great deal of pressure, of both the moral and political kind.

In March 1964 he voted against pay raises for Congress, including, of course, his own (House members, be it said, were then paid the munificent salary of $22,500 plus a modest allowance to cover one or two trips a year to visit their constituents). In the following month he called the agreement for the United States to sell

---

[1] The problem of America's defense and management of "inner space" would remain an issue at the forefront of Rumsfeldian concern: In the year 2000 he would become chairman of a commission to assess the problem of U.S. National Security space management at the behest of the U.S. House of Representatives Committee on Armed Services.

wheat to the Soviet Union "the most colossal blunder in recent years."

In September, during his reelection campaign, he made a great point of attacking Soviet persecution of the Jews, while also presenting a resolution to that effect in the House. And come November, he once again beat his Democratic opponent handily. But with Lyndon Johnson's landslide victory over Barry Goldwater that same month, he was one of only 140 Republican Congressmen left standing—or, if you will, sitting.

It was around this time that a group of these survivors, with Rumsfeld himself very much in the lead, began to occupy themselves with the problem of how to reinvigorate the Republican party in the House. This group came to be known as "Rumsfeld's Raiders," and one of its main ambitions was to put in place a much broader distribution of party responsibilities than the Republican old guard in the House had seen fit to allow. The minority leader, one Charles Halleck of Indiana, was regarded by Rumsfeld's Raiders as one of the chief impediments to the kind of changes they hoped to bring about. One of their demands was that at least ten positions of responsibility should be opened up to the younger members. Halleck was desperate to keep his job, and made some effort to placate the group, but in the end he seemed not to understand just how serious the demand being put to him was. In a move that would turn out to be a fateful one for Rumsfeld's future, he pushed for the election to minority leader of a certain very popular colleague named Gerald Ford. And on January 4, 1965, Ford won.

Under the new minority leader, Rumsfeld continued to make his presence felt in the chambers of the House—indeed, he would continue to do so for all the five years now remaining to him there. Some of his more notable stands, among the many that were defined and defended by him over those years, were: calling for a study of the practices of the House Un-American Activities Committee; accusing the John Birch Society of having "lazy minds" and "always looking for simple answers to very complex problems"; opposing American aid to Nasser on the ground that the Egyptian dictator could use such aid to aggress against various countries in the Middle East; and proposing tax credits for college admission, as well as for businesses engaged in training or retrain-

ing their lesser-skilled employees. He also supported the Freedom of Information Act, the creation of a Department of Transportation, tax credits for antipollution devices, a truth-in-lending bill, and the 1968 civil rights bill. In mid-June of 1967 he urged the United States to refrain from demanding Israeli withdrawal from territories conquered in the Six-Day War, and later, in September of that year, he deplored the delay in the United States delivery of Skyhawk bombers to the Israelis.

But in its way the most interesting, not to say ultimately the most fateful, of his positions was his early and unwavering opposition to the draft. This might at first have seemed an unlikely position for someone of his generation and upbringing (and there are those among his friends and allies who to this day do not agree with him about this). His argument was—and is—basically twofold. First, since the army cannot make use of everyone eligible to be drafted, the system is inherently unfair: only some of the eligible will be taken and required to serve, while the others will be able to find easier, more comfortable, and better-paying work to do. And second, having so easily available a source of manpower is very wasteful: At that point, for instance—in the mid-sixties—there were some 9,000 enlisted men engaged in such entirely nonmilitary duties as working in officers' clubs, hobby shops, bowling alleys, golf courses, commissary sales stores, and so on. It was better, he believed, to have an army made up of people who volunteered to serve. (Rumsfeld would never waver on this issue, from that time until today. Though nearly four decades after he first made this argument, he would be excoriated for having been thought to say that the Vietnam War draftees provided no advan-

Later: Marcy (left) would "sleep on things" and Valerie would prefer Illinois.

tage to the armed forces, when it was the means by which they had been made to serve, rather than their service itself, that he had been talking about.)

But as might have been expected by those who had known him in his early years, not all the dramatic clashes of his life were even then confined to his battles on Capitol Hill. At times, he might have seemed to be a magnet for drama. Some time during the evening of October 28, 1963, for instance, as he was driving home

he happened on a group of policemen in hot pursuit of a reckless young drag racer. When the young man attempted to escape by jumping out of his car, Rumsfeld stopped his own car, jumped out himself, tackled the fugitive, and held him until the police could take over. The incident was, as may be imagined, taken due note of by the Washington press.

Over the remaining years of his tenure in Congress he continued to advocate policies that would make him rather difficult to place on any Left-Right continuum. Thus, until it passed in June 1966, he persisted in supporting the Freedom of Information Act, hardly a measure to gladden the hearts of conservatives. Nor could his views on Vietnam, which he visited around the same time, have done so. For on his return he announced that winning the war would not by a long shot solve the Vietnam problem. On the other hand, he was a firm advocate of fiscal responsibility, and also believed in tax credits for such things as antipollution devices and books, tuition, and fees for college. In 1966—something that would cast a most interesting shadow on his future—he supported a bill called the "Opportunity Crusade Act," which was an effort to put a more conservative spin on the "war on poverty" recently declared by President Lyndon Johnson. This was a bill for reorganizing the Office of Economic Opportunity—the agency created by Johnson as one of the main engines of that war—so that there would be greater emphasis placed on educational programs like Head Start and on-the-job training for the unskilled. Another provision of this bill—which, needless to say, did not pass—was that it would have permitted the elderly to work without losing Social Security.

Father and son, Nicholas, at work

IN THE spring of 1968, Rumsfeld announced his intention to run for a fourth term. Then during the following August, he attended the Republican convention in Miami and served there as a floor manager for Richard Nixon. After the convention Nixon appointed him to be a member of what he called his "Flying Truth Squad"—a group of spokesmen delegated to travel around and act as surrogate candidates in the upcoming presidential campaign. His own fourth run for office (as it would turn out, his last) promised to be a sure thing, which freed him up to engage in a good deal of campaigning as a spokesman for Nixon. And come November not only was Nixon victorious but Rumsfeld carried his district by one of the largest percentages in the nation.

Meanwhile, however, all had now become far from sweetness and light for him in the House. Though Ford was now minority leader, that move by itself had not guaranteed all the reforms Rumsfeld's Raiders were after, and for Rumsfeld himself there was an added difficulty: The unseating of Halleck had much displeased Representative Leslie Arends, the Republican whip who happened to be the dean of the Illinois congressional delegation as well as a friend and supporter of Halleck's. Thus by January of 1969, when a move, this time to unseat Arends, had been tried and failed, Rumsfeld was in some trouble. (If you go after the king, as the old saying has it, you had better make sure to kill him.) When it proved impossible to drag congressional reforms out of the House Rules Committee and bring them to the floor, and when he also lost his bid for a committee chairmanship that had been very important to him, he began, as *Time* magazine put it, to feel "cramped."

From his earliest days in Congress Rumsfeld had taken part in an ongoing struggle to achieve the redistribution of Republican congressional power. But now it seemed clear that for the foreseeable future—with Congress firmly in Democratic hands—there was going to be precious little of such power available to the Republicans for any kind of redistribution. To a man so very much built for action, this was bound to be a seriously troubling prospect.

"I always *loved* working on the Hill," he says. "But we were in the minority, and it looked like we were going to be in the minority for a long time. I had helped Gerald Ford run for minority leader, and in the process had angered Les Arends. So there was a happy Gerald Ford and an unhappy Les Arends. . . . ."

WHEREUPON ENTER Richard Nixon, bearing gifts. In April, three months after his inauguration, Nixon invited Rumsfeld to the White House and asked him to become the new head of the Office of Economic Opportunity. Rumsfeld at first declined, on the ground that as a congressman he had voted against establishing the OEO and had then supported the Opportunity Crusade Act, which was intended to alter it. "That," replied the newly seated president, "is exactly why we want you."

"Then he hit me again, and I said yes. I found it a heck of a challenge—my first executive assignment." This time Nixon's "hit" had included sweetening the pot by offering the title of assistant to the president with cabinet rank along with the directorship of OEO. All in all, the offer was one that could not have been refused for long—and besides, he could always imagine, or at least hope, that there would be some way to bring the agency he had opposed to the point of serving some kind of worthwhile purpose.

In late May, Rumsfeld was confirmed as head of OEO by the Senate. There now began a round of making new connections and friendships that would—as in the case of New Trier and Princeton—be fated to go on, as it were, forever. "It's important to me to work with people who have a sense of humor—so that it can be comfortable to work for long hours." Among those he brought to work for him were a young former academic named Richard Cheney. Another was a young lawyer named Frank Carlucci (who had also been a wrestler at Princeton, as well as the roommate in law school of Rumsfeld's dear friend John Robson, and who would one day become secretary of defense during the second term of

President Ronald Reagan). Then there was Kenneth Adelman and his future wife, Carol (a graduate student at Georgetown, who had come with Don to OEO from his congressional office). After a while two young interns, one a recent graduate of Wheaton College named Christie Todd—later to become Christie Todd Whitman—and the other an all-American basketball player from Princeton named Bill Bradley, would spend some time hanging out at OEO. (Rumsfeld never ceased believing that Bradley should have been a Republican.) He also appointed Terry Lenzner to be the director of the agency's legal services department, but in this case, far from cementing a friendship, the appointment would soon bring unhappiness all around, and with a little prodding from Nixon, it would end in a parting of the ways. For Lenzner had enthusiastically embraced much of the ethos of the radical "anti-poverty" community, thereby making not only President Nixon but also California's Governor Ronald Reagan very unhappy with him.

"I kept finding that I thought I knew more than I knew," Rumsfeld laughs. "I studied government in college and served as a congressional staff member, and then, of course, in Congress, and I had every reason to believe that I knew how the government worked. But when I left the legislative branch and saw the way the executive branch really worked—which was so different from what I had thought as a student or a staffperson or a congressman—I had a whole new education. And to be able to spend time at the White House at the same time as I was running OEO, to see both ends of that rubber band, was fascinating."

Out of Congress and into the White House: Justice Warren Burger swears in the new director.

When Rumsfeld arrived at OEO, he discovered a situation more out of control than even he, for all his early opposition, had imagined. The agency was basically a hotbed for the preaching and teaching of "community action"—a euphemism for stirring up radical opposition, in the name of the poor, to a whole variety of forms of government authority. Frank Carlucci would in later years speak to interviewers of his shock when, on going through OEO's offices for the first time, he found the walls plastered with posters of Che Guevara and other equally lively examples of what the Communists used to call agitprop. Next it was discovered that pamphlets and other material were being circulated among community-action groups funded by OEO that advocated demonstrations, boycotts, and, if necessary, violence as legitimate weapons of the poor against their governmental oppressors.

Taking over in the middle of all this, Rumsfeld devised for himself a policy that, he believed (or perhaps only hoped), would provide him with a means for bringing the agency under control. That is, he decided that under his direction OEO would become a kind of experimental laboratory whose successful programs, should there be any, could then be distributed among the various relevant government agencies and departments. He would act on this new policy by "delegating" the Head Start program—long regarded as the greatest success of the anti-poverty initiatives—to the department of Health, Education, and Welfare.

As a further sign of the agency's being under new and different management, he served notice that, beginning with the city of Minneapolis and, if need be, going on from there, OEO would cut

Counselor to the president meets with Anwar Sadat

off all funding for those radical activists who had seized control of community-action programs. But in truth, he was up against nothing less mighty than a cultural tidal wave: one, moreover, to which his president, with other things on his mind, was basically ready to surrender. Except perhaps here and there at the margins, it seems unlikely that the Office of Economic Opportunity progressed very far in the direction of reform, let alone transformation.

Still, the Donald Rumsfeld who was assistant to the president was once again learning to find his way, this time through and around the White House. Among other things, he made the acquaintance, and no doubt took the measure, of Nixon's national security adviser, Henry Kissinger; befriended his domestic policy adviser (one day to be senator), Daniel P. Moynihan; and grew ever more uncomfortable with Nixon's inner circle of staff and confidants.

Then, just a little more than two years after Rumsfeld's arrival at OEO, Nixon announced the establishment of a Cost of Living Council, which was a relatively harmless-sounding euphemism for the federal imposition of wage-and-price controls. Employment was down and inflation was rising, and Nixon, convinced that Kennedy had beat him by a hair in 1962 because of a softening economy, was now worried about reelection.

Again he asked Rumsfeld to head the program, again Rumsfeld protested that he was in principle opposed to it, and again the president told him that this was precisely why he would be the best man to administer it.

Initially the system seemed to be working, and after three months the controls were gradually relaxed. But not for long: As it turned out, unemployment was not actually declining and inflation was beginning to pick up again. One night, as Rumsfeld tells it, he came home late, reached into the refrigerator for a beer, and found a note that Joyce had taped onto the door. The note said:

> *He tackled a job that couldn't be done,*
> *With a smile, he went right to it.*
> *He tackled a job that couldn't be done,*
> *And couldn't do it.*

The Cost of Living Council would not actually be abolished until April 1974 (seventeen months after Nixon was reelected and only four months before he was forced to resign from the presidency).

By that time, however, the Rumsfelds would be living in Brussels, and for Don it would be his first—but as fate would have it, far from his last—taste of Europe and the Europeans.

3

MOVING ON

T HE QUESTION is: How did Donald Rumsfeld come to seek the United States ambassadorship to NATO—the job that took him far away from the White House—in February of 1973, a time when the scandal of Watergate would be making its way ever more dangerously close to the president himself?

It is true that Rumsfeld had long been less than comfortable with Nixon's inmost circle—H. R. Haldeman, John Ehrlichman, and company—not to mention the personal friends with whom Nixon preferred to relax. Did he, then, cleverly conclude that the political operatives in the White House, and perhaps even the president himself, had ultimately been responsible for Watergate, or at least the crime of covering up Watergate, and that it would be the

Reviewing NATO troops

better part of wisdom to find himself a spot somewhere out of town? Or was it that, in accordance with some inner Rumsfeldian time clock, he had learned what there was for him to learn from this White House and so felt that it was now time to be moving on?

The answer is, both of the above. But there was something else moving in him as well, and that was an ever growing interest in foreign affairs. This interest, though it was evident in many of his positions and speeches, had been granted rather limited scope in his time as a congressman: outside, in the streets and classrooms of America, a kind of civil war over Vietnam was being waged. But inside the halls of Congress the Republicans were largely preoccupied with other matters. Subsequently, neither the Office of Economic Opportunity nor the Cost of Living Council afforded him much time for questions of American foreign and defense policy. As he would tell an interviewer about the importance to him of his year and a half spent in Brussels, "At NATO I was reading different books, worrying about different problems, living with different kinds of people, thinking about different things."

By then the Cold War had been in progress for more than twenty years, with its ultimately most controversial offshoot, the Vietnam War, whimpering to a sad and sorry close. Beyond this American entanglement in what had come to be characterized as a "quagmire," certain of the countries of Western Europe—America's NATO allies—were showing signs of weariness with the need to keep their powder forever dry. Meanwhile, Nixon and Secretary of State Henry Kissinger were intent upon achieving a new era of detente with the Soviet Union. At the same time, military technology was becoming ever more sophisticated and dangerous. In response to all this Rumsfeld now wanted to turn his full attention to the realm of national security and foreign affairs.

And so it was that in December of 1972, six months after the break-in at the Watergate, Rumsfeld got himself appointed the

United States ambassador to NATO. Two months later he was confirmed and on his way to Brussels. For the Rumsfelds, Brussels would be the gateway to a widening of experience, bringing with it new preoccupations and new horizons. And though the ambassadorial residence in Brussels, like many another Rumsfeld domicile, would turn out to be a short-lived address, for Don in particular the move worked a significant shift in the whole course of his future life.

VALERIE RUMSFELD was now seventeen years old, Marcy, thirteen, and Nicholas, six, which meant among other things that one of the issues now facing the Rumsfelds would be what to do about the children's schooling. Valerie, for instance, was at that point a junior in high school; it would be essential not to disrupt her preparation for college. She had, in fact, asked if she might stay behind in Washington so that she could complete her senior year and from there also go about the business of applying to college. This proposal was greeted with an instantaneous and firm not on your life, we are a family and we will go on living as a family in Brussels. (Valerie would later express gratitude for her parents' refusal to countenance the idea that she remain behind in America, saying that the family's adventures in Europe had been not only a most enjoyable but an immensely important experience for her.) It was decided, then, that in order not to make things difficult for her so close to graduation, Valerie would attend the school in Brussels being conducted in English and in accordance with American standards by the Department of Defense.

Nicholas, on the other hand, who was just going into kindergarten and was at an age when a change of language would come easily, was sent to a local Belgian school, while Marcy, in between, was given her choice. Feeling uncomfortable about being the ambassador's child in the Department of Defense school (she had visited the place with Valerie and said that too much attention was being paid to her on account of her father), she decided instead to go where her little brother was going. This proved to be extremely difficult, because in the small local institution she had opted for no allowance could be made for the fact that she knew no French. Which meant that, as was so characteristically put to her by her father, "Of all the kids in your classroom you are the one who will have to pay the closest attention." As she remembers it, each day as she arrived home for lunch she would be positively white with exhaustion from the strain of trying to concentrate on what was being discussed in a language she was only beginning to understand and was not yet brave enough to attempt to speak. And each day her mother would look at the state she was in and say, "Now, we are not going to cry, because if we start crying, you will never make it back today."

There was also some concern about the safety of the Rumsfeld children: Rumors of a possible kidnapping were making the rounds in Brussels. As characteristic on her part as the advice to Marcy about paying attention had been on her husband's, Joyce, who was indeed worried, did not want the children to feel threatened. So for weeks as they walked to school each morning she walked a block or two behind them in order to make sure that they were safe without their seeing her.

As for the ambassador himself, along with gaining a deepened sense of both the Europeans and their foreign and military affairs, he would once again make some new friends (and, to join the Hallecks and the Arendses, some new enemies as well).

Joyce and Nicholas, European travelers

Beyond this, there was the seeing, feeling, tasting of Europe. The Rumsfeld family spent the ambassador's free time traveling around, sometimes meeting up—as they would continue all through their lives to do—with old friends from America. One of these reunions, with the Jannottas, included a visit to Pamplona to witness the famous running of the bulls. While the two families found a second-story perch from which to witness the proceedings in the street beneath them, Don had been unable to resist the call of adventure and had remained below. As the bulls came thundering down the street in the direction of the building from which

they were watching, they saw him running along with the crowd of young blades who turn up each year to rile the bulls and then test their own mettle in eluding the animals' growing rage. And just as the bulls were within hot-breath range of the forty-one-year-old foreign dignitary, he leaped up, grabbed hold of a lamppost, and hung there until the stampede had passed. (As more and more people would come to discover over the years, it is no easy thing— even for a bull—to win out with someone who is always at the ready for a testing.)

The Rumsfeldian European idyll would come to a rather speedy end (as perhaps idylls, before they become routines, are meant to do). For in the late summer and early fall of 1974 two things happened that once again changed the course of all their lives.

The first of these was that on August 9 of that year Richard Nixon resigned from the presidency and Rumsfeld's old friend and ally Gerald Ford, then vice president, was sworn in as the new president. And one of the first actions Ford took as president was send to Brussels for Rumsfeld and ask him to put together a transition team for the new White House. Many of Nixon's old staff were still around, and Ford naturally wanted to surround himself with people of his own. Thus getting it all sorted out would require a highly skilled operation, and his old ally from their days in the House was just the man to undertake it.

Rumsfeld, back in Washington for what he imagined would be only a temporary stay, believed that this transition team should function for at most only thirty days. Otherwise, he feared, there would be two groups of people trying to run the White House and

With Kissinger in Canada, June 1974

making more than a double amount of trouble and confusion. (In the event, he found that he and his team were able to finish up in only two weeks.) Under Nixon, the White House staff had ballooned from 250 to 540, and among the things the Rumsfeld group recommended was a serious cutback in personnel. Beyond sorting out and reducing the size of his staff, however, Ford aspired to do something more radical. Spooked by what had been revealed about the various conspiratorial workings of the Nixon White House, he wanted to institute what he called an "open door presidency." Which meant, first and foremost, eliminating the office of White House chief of staff so that no one would have the power to regulate his time and prevent him from maintaining contact with people whose company he might for one reason or another consider valuable.

But before long Ford was forced to change his mind, and this led to yet another radical turning in the course of Rumsfeld's life and career. During the September after Don's brief sojourn in Washington to help with the transition, his father, who had for some time been suffering from Alzheimer's disease, died. While in Illinois for the funeral, Don received a second urgent call from Ford: Please, could he come to Washington right away? Turning up at the White House the next day, he was asked by Ford if he would be willing to serve as chief of staff. (Whether or not this question was put sheepishly, coming so soon after the president's insistence that there be no such job in his White House, was never recorded.) The "open door" had proved to be far too uncontrollably open and the volume of traffic through it was actually interfering with the work of the presidency. Rumsfeld answered that he would be reluctant to take on the job unless he were given full authority to run the White House's administrative machinery—in other words, precisely what Ford had hoped to avoid. But having experienced the impracticality of his original ambition, Ford now agreed to Rumsfeld's terms.

Thus the Rumsfelds once again returned to Washington, and with Dick Cheney as his deputy, Don soon found an even greater scope for all his various energies—political, managerial, and intellectual. In doing so, he ruffled more than a few feathers: Those, for example, of Nixon's—and subsequently Ford's—national security adviser/secretary of state, Henry Kissinger[1]; William Simon, then secretary of the treasury, a man not noted for his cheerfulness at being prevented from doing what he believed needed to be done—or for that matter, even sometimes simply at being disagreed with; Nelson Rockefeller, whom Ford had named to be his vice president soon after ascending to the presidency and who, when asked to resign only a little more than a year later, held Rumsfeld responsible; and finally, George H. W. Bush, the man who would always believe that Rumsfeld was behind his so desperately unwanted appointment to the CIA.

Of course, making enemies is not a difficult thing to do in Washington. In any capital, as in any royal court, there is always much more hunger—for power, for perks, for status—than can ever be satisfied, and Washington was now, so to speak, the capital of capitals. Having been a congressman—a congressman, moreover, who had played a leading role in toppling his own minority leader—as well as the head of a government agency and a member of the Cabinet, Rumsfeld had already earned his share of hostility.

---

[1] In his memoir of the Ford administration, *Years of Renewal,* published in 1999, Kissinger would heap praise on Rumsfeld and express some regret that someone with such great political gifts should in the end have failed to pursue the presidency. At the time, however, this seemed to have been rather far from Kissinger's view of the matter.

In any case, despite his denials, then and now, he was widely assumed to be pulling the strings when, on October 25, 1975, Gerald Ford met with Kissinger and informed him that he was about to make a series of changes in the administration. The first of these would be the dumping of Rockefeller, who it was feared would prove a liability on the ticket for the next year's election. Then, a

Above: *Amid teacups, back in Washington once more*

few days after Rockefeller's resignation, in what the press immediately and with the usual journalistic glee dubbed "The Halloween Massacre," Ford fired secretary of defense James Schlesinger and CIA Director William Colby, relieved Kissinger of his dual role as secretary of state and national security advisor, thereby sending him out of the White House and off to the Department of State, and elevated Kissinger's deputy, Brent Scowcroft, to his former White House job. Further, not only did George Bush become director of the CIA but Donald Rumsfeld replaced James Schlesinger at the Pentagon, with Dick Cheney taking Rumsfeld's place as White House chief of staff. Having done all this, Ford could now begin to work seriously on his upcoming, and in the end ill-fated, presidential campaign.

Aside from the question of whether or not Rumsfeld had had a hand in all the changes that stirred so much hard feeling against him, what Rumsfeld actually thought of them has never been recorded. He did not then—nor does he to this day—make use of the press to further his interoffice opinions or ambitions, as others have done so effectively and for so long. The one exception in the case of the "Halloween Massacre" was Ford's firing of Schlesinger, a move of which Rumsfeld disapproved—though he himself was its beneficiary—on the grounds that if Ford had been unhappy with this particular inheritance from the Nixon administration[2], the change should have been made immediately upon his taking office or should at least have waited until after his reelection.

In any case, Schlesinger's departure at first left the powers that

---

[2] Ford, it seems, had never been comfortable with Schlesinger, and according to Kissinger had once said to him, "[Schlesinger] thinks I am stupid, and he believes you are running me, which he resents. This conflict will not end until I either fire Jim or make him believe *he* is running me."

be in the Pentagon feeling both unhappy and suspicious, for they regarded the now-deposed secretary as a true ally. Known around the Pentagon as "the Professor," Schlesinger had provided them with much of the intellectual, and perhaps even the emotional, wherewithal to rebuild and regroup after the Vietnam War. Moreover, while they were still suffering from the demoralization of a once unimaginable defeat in those far-off jungles, they now had to make the very large adjustment involved in learning to preside over an all-volunteer army. Furthermore, when it came to practicalities, Schlesinger had sought to help them (albeit without

any very resounding success) in their battle against a Congress then hell-bent on slashing their budgets. To top all this off, over the course of only seven years there had already been three secretaries of defense—Melvin Laird, Elliot Richardson, and James Schlesinger—and Rumsfeld would now make the fourth. (He would also, which may not have been all that reassuring, be the youngest in history.)

The Pentagonians did, however, take some comfort from the idea that Rumsfeld clearly had the ear of the president. And before long they would recognize that, quite apart from his connection to the White House, he was no less an ally than his predecessor. It also helped that Martin Hoffman, the old Princeton classmate with whom Rumsfeld happened to have been breakfasting when he interrupted himself to rush off and propose to Joyce, was then secretary of the army. Together the two men managed either to sort out, or to set aside, more than one Vietnam hangover.

D URING RUMSFELD'S first tour as secretary of defense there were basically two main issues agitating foreign and defense policy. One was whether, and/or what, to negotiate with the Soviets in the way of an arms agreement. In Nixon's first term—that is, beginning in 1969—Nixon and Kissinger had worked on the first Strategic Arms Limitation Treaty (SALT I), which was signed in 1972. Many members of the military had been unhappy about SALT I, but this was the time when the United States was engaged in extricating itself from the Vietnam War and easing tensions with

With Ford on Air Force One

the Soviets was immensely popular throughout the country, on the Right as well as on the Left.

Immediately after securing Brezhnev's signature on SALT I, Nixon and Kissinger had begun negotiating the treaty known as SALT II; it was around this negotiation that an active and increasingly noisy opposition, both military and civilian, had solidified. This opposition was based essentially on two main objections: One,

Above: With Dick Cheney (left) and Ford in the Oval Office

that the terms of SALT II were advantageous to the Soviets and disadvantageous to the United States, and two, that even so, the Soviets were even then actively preparing to violate the agreement.

Another issue had to do with the question of whether Congress would be willing to fund both the kind and amount of new equipment and weapons the military judged necessary to insure American security. The two issues were naturally closely related, for the belief that SALT I would help bring about a relaxation of the arms race had also done much to relax Congress about the need for keeping up its expenditures on the military budget.

Though as a matter of principle Rumsfeld did not then (nor does he now) publicly express disagreement with the president in whose administration he served (and serves), it was an open secret that he and the joint chiefs of staff opposed Kissinger's efforts to get a second SALT treaty. Ford tried, but found himself unable, to adjudicate this dispute between his secretaries of state and defense. To judge from his memoir, *A Time to Heal,* it would seem that in the end he did not fully understand what the dispute was really about, namely, the country's general posture with respect to what the opponents of the SALT II treaty declared was a massive Soviet arms buildup. For the book characterizes the objections raised by Rumsfeld and the joint chiefs as merely "highly technical."[3]

Rumsfeld was also careful never to speak ill of detente with the Soviets, the policy that was associated first and foremost with the name of Kissinger both by those who supported it and those who were passionately opposed. Instead, when forced to express his view, Rumsfeld would merely lighten and aerate the concept of de-

---

[3] When Ford gave Rumsfeld a copy of the book, he said he believed that Rumsfeld wouldn't like it because in the book he held Rumsfeld at least partly responsible for the defeat of SALT II—clearly unaware that this might please, rather than displease, his one-time secretary of defense.

Sharing a light moment with Henry Kissinger, President Ford, and Alan Greenspan

tente by describing it to be no more than an effort to relax tension between the two great powers. (This was a technique for setting aside a possibly nonnegotiable conflict of opinion that he would bring to a state of high polish during his second tour at the Pentagon.) But for those who knew, and others inclined to listen carefully to both the words and the music of what he was saying,

there could be no doubt that like his predecessor, Rumsfeld stood with the hard-line Cold Warriors.

Moreover, however tactful the secretary of defense might try to be in couching his opinions, during January of 1975 the Pentagon issued what is called the Annual Posture Statement. This particular document, to which Rumsfeld had certainly given his most careful scrutiny, declared that "The U.S. effort must be as serious, as steady and sustained, as that of the Soviet Union." Further, the United States must be prepared to fight a limited nuclear war as well as deter an all-out one, and must build new "blockbuster ICBM's, strategic bombers, and a fleet of warships." Hardly the view of an institution in the mood to give a warm, or even a cold, embrace to the reduction of strategic arms.

One priority for this posture, in Rumsfeld's view, was the development of the B-1 bomber. The B-1 was, and would remain, both a mightily expensive and highly controversial aircraft. The former navy pilot believed in it, however, and fought for it. Indeed, in April of 1976, in order to discredit the rumors of the plane's unreliability that had been feeding the opposition to it in the Senate, and though he himself had learned to fly before the age of jets, he set out to demonstrate the superior capabilities of the B-1 by piloting it over the California desert for fifty minutes.

As he traveled around the country giving speeches and press conferences, there were two main points Rumsfeld stressed over and over. The first was, as he put it, that "the greatest threat to the relationship between the United States and the Soviet Union is not . . . belligerency. . . . [T]he greatest danger historically to free

Ford and the Rumsfelds: (left to right) *Marcy, Joyce, Nicholas, Valerie, and Don*

people is that during periods of relative peace and stability . . . there has been a tendency . . . to relax . . . and to become weak. And we know, historically, that weakness can be just as provocative as belligerence."

Above: *Swearing in the new, and youngest, Secretary of Defense, November 20, 1975*

The second point he made was in answer to complaints about the size of the military budget. Both in constant dollars and as a percentage of the total budget, he explained, the country's spending on the military had been going down, not up. In addition, he insisted that what ought to concern both the Congress and the people was not only America's military capability at that particular moment but what it would be in the years ahead. For while our own military budget had been declining, that of the Soviet Union had been steadily growing.

Perhaps because the military was beginning to come up through the ice, or perhaps because the youngest secretary of defense not only had the ear of the president but also still retained many of his old contacts in Congress, or perhaps both, the military budget of 1976 at least marked the end of the downward trend. The budget of 1977 would even reflect some small but real growth.

THE 1976 presidential election turned the White House over to the Democrats in the person of James Earl Carter, and Inauguration Day—January 20, 1977—found Rumsfeld once again packing up and on the move. He was now forty-four years old. In a little more than eight years he had held five different jobs of ever-increasing prominence and responsibility. He had also called upon and intensified old friendships and alliances and had solidified new ones. Under Nixon, he had gained what had to have been a valuable acquaintance with the sordid side of life, hardly matched even by his experience in Congress. Apart from Watergate, there had been the illicit hijinks of the activists being supported by the Office of Economic Opportunity, and there were, inevitably, a few of the less than admirable diplomatic shenanigans he encountered in

Brussels. Then under Ford he had been given his greatest opportunity so far to cultivate a long-developing appetite for heavy and ever heavier responsibility.

And something else: The thirteenth secretary of defense had on a number of occasions been required to hold press conferences. On these occasions he had done a certain amount of jousting with reporters and others, sometimes humorous and sometimes rather more intense. No evidence has been left behind as to whether or not his questioners enjoyed the experience, but a reading of the transcripts of these press conferences makes it perfectly—the word perhaps is *prophetically*—evident that *he* did.

All this added up to a very large number of careers for someone who had barely passed the middle of the journey. And there would be a number more to come.

Above: *with Charles Lindbergh,* (left) *and Laurence Rockefeller*

Right: *April 1976: flying the B-1 bomber to prove its reliability*

4

TAKING CHARGE

I T USED to be said in Washington that when the Republicans are out of office they go home to where they came from whereas the Democrats always stick around waiting for the chance to return to power. That may no longer be true (if it ever was), but there seemed little doubt that with Ford out of office the Rumsfelds would soon be heading back to Winnetka.

During that first spring, however, now freed from the constraints of being a member of Gerald Ford's team and thus somewhat careful in his public discussions of our relations with the Soviet Union, Rumsfeld spent some time going around the country—as he would continue to do in the years ahead—speaking out against the seductions of arms control ("thinking that if we disarm the Soviets will follow").

Welcoming Saudi Prince Abdullah to the Pentagon

In addition, he was a visiting lecturer at his alma mater Princeton, and he also taught two courses in government management at Northwestern. But apart from its appeal to him as a chance to do some serious reading and thinking out from under the pressure of daily hard decision-making, the academic life in the end held little attraction for him. Because it was precisely under Washington-style pressure—or some other pressure like it—that the former newsboy-Eagle Scout-wrestler-navy pilot would always find himself most alive and at ease.

In any case, by April of 1977 the Chicago press began to carry stories suggesting that there was about to be yet another career for Rumsfeld, one that would present him with a new and distinctly different world to map and master. And indeed, it was shortly announced that on June 1 he would become the president and chief executive officer of the Searle Pharmaceutical Company of Skokie, Illinois.

The company, an old family firm then being run by two Searle brothers, Dan and William, and their brother-in-law, Wesley Dixon, had fallen on rather hard times. Sales of Searle's products were up, but for more than a year the company's profits had been declining. Moreover, the animal studies that had been submitted to the Food and Drug Administration in support of Searle's two new diuretics, Aldactone and Aldactazine, had been found so flawed as to make it impossible to determine whether or not they might be toxic—so flawed, indeed, that the FDA had even called for a grand jury to investigate the company. In the face of all this, the price of Searle stock had now fallen to $10 from its 1973 high of $41.

The Searles had known and admired Don since his days as a congressman (Dan Searle had been an early supporter) and were full of hope that he could do something to turn the company around. Jeanette Rumsfeld, on the other hand, was dead set against

her son's taking the job. You now have such a good reputation, why risk it, Jeanette warned him, by trying to run a business you know nothing about, a business that is even under investigation by a grand jury! As it inevitably would, and fortunately for both the Searles and the Rumsfelds, this maternal warning fell on deaf ears.

Beyond turning their company over to someone whom others in the business community must surely have considered a mere amateur, the Searles and Wesley Dixon did something else quite extraordinary, if not, indeed, almost unheard of in the annals of business: In order not only not to interfere but to be *seen* as not interfering, they moved out of their offices at Searle and into another building. Whereupon this gesture of confidence was answered by the new CEO with a gesture of his own in a similar spirit. He set aside a place for a master file containing each and every bit of important paper produced under his management and he then announced to the Searles and Dixon that the file had been expressly created for them and they could come around and go through it whenever they wished. Whatever would be the future lot of the Searle company under its new CEO, then, it is unlikely that there could anywhere in the annals of American business have been an instance of more handsome relations between a company's retired owners and its new management.

Rumsfeld spent from April to June—two months—studying the business and then took over. By September he was ready to move on what seemed to him one of Searle's major problems: the operation had become too centralized and too focused on corporate headquarters rather than on the company's actual business, which was the research into and production of pharmaceuticals. He then set about to remedy the situation by firing 150 employees outright and transferring 150 others from the corporate staff to the various groups that were actually in charge of producing and selling Searle's various product lines. (In addition to achieving what he felt was the necessary decentralization, this move was to save the company some five million dollars.)

Henry Kissinger had once characterized Rumsfeld as ruthless ("ruthless" being a term of art in the White House, applied to someone whose strength of mind is used in opposition to, rather than in support of, yours). No one of importance at the Pentagon seems to have leveled this charge during his first tour of duty there, but at the time the military were having far more serious problems than the secretary could have had time to make for them. At Searle, however—certainly among those three hundred employees whose lives he had with so much dispatch turned upside down, but among others as well—a heavy load of hard feelings was quickly collected, followed inevitably by a full measure of nasty stories.

After all, whatever else it might be, a business whose corporate headquarters are steadily being expanded is a place of comfort. And through this warm place the new CEO had, in virtually no time and with no hesitation, sent a cold, cold wind. It is said that he had come to be known there as "the axman." (The other side of this coin, of course, is the feeling of security experienced by people when they recognize that they are working for someone who knows what he is doing.)

Soon after, he again did something that few CEOs with formal business training might have thought—or dared—to do: He sent for his old friend, John Robson, whose life, like his own, had thus far been spent exclusively in public service, "jawboning" about economics in the Johnson White House, serving first as general counsel to the Department of Transportation and later to the Civil Aeronautics Board. At the time Rumsfeld summoned him to Searle, Robson was a fellow of the American Enterprise Institute, a Washington think tank. "You had better come out here," Don told him. "There's a lot to do here."

Robson, who had been issues director in Rumsfeld's first congressional campaign, was in some ways very different from and very much a complement to his new boss: a man who loved to dance, for instance, and who, like Joyce, was passionate about music and the arts. As a lawyer with experience in the fields of economics and government regulation, he would play a far more important role in the business than that of counselor. He would, in fact, be Rumsfeld's right hand—and would later replace him as CEO.

The following winter Rumsfeld brought in James Denny to serve as chief financial officer. Denny, though not then the close

Talking about Searle Pharmaceuticals: James Denny (left), Rumsfeld, and John Robson

friend he was soon to become, happened also to have been a member of the Princeton class of 1954. Before coming to Searle, he had been working in Akron for the Firestone Tire Company, which was then in some financial trouble, and Rumsfeld never tired of claiming that he had been Denny's rescuer. (Later the three men would create a partnership for the purpose of doing some investing. This partnership would be called TBM—which stands for Three Blind Mice.)

"When I went to Searle," Rumsfeld says, "I was interested in the private sector. And it turned out I had really been thinking about it one-dimensionally. I didn't understand it as I needed to, that is, three-dimensionally. A government agency or a congressional committee can delay something for a week or a month or a year. And I had not understood, for example, what kind of impact such delays had on a large company as against a small company. A large company has lawyers, lobbyists, and so on—in other words, has sufficient heft that a delay isn't quite so costly. It *is* costly, of course, but the problem is masked by this mass. But a small company it sucks the life out of. A six-month delay on whether or not the government is going to renew something, say, a tax exemption for Puerto Rico, makes it difficult for a company. Where are you going to put a new plant, for instance? Congressional committees hold hearings, and uncertainty is exactly what increases their PACs and draws the money in. There were so many things like that that I really didn't understand. To get into a business and get a sense of the effect of the things we had been taking for granted in Congress was just fascinating."

A S FAR as Searle in particular was concerned, the new CEO had worked hard at learning its ways, and he was now prepared to scale back the result of what had been a heedless and costly belief in the efficacy of mere acquisition. Thus he proceeded to divest the company of some twenty businesses, mostly in the area of hospital and diagnostic products, that together accounted for about $100 million of the $800 million of Searle's sales. This, observed the *Wall Street Journal,* "will put Searle considerably into the red for the year." (Which it did, but, as Rumsfeld had hoped and believed, during the following year the company would post earnings of $72.2 million—as compared with a loss of more than $28 million in 1977.)

As things turned out, however, not all of Searle's hospital-supply businesses proved to be worth getting rid of. One of them, Will Ross, Inc., had moved into the area of retail eyeglasses and contact lenses and in a chain of stores called Vision Centers had been growing quite rapidly. Rumsfeld separated Vision Centers from the hospital supplier, expanded it, and with considerable satisfaction—and perhaps even a touch of amusement—watched as it became Searle's fastest growing business.

Beyond the issues of heedless diversification and improperly presented research, the company had also reached the point where the patents of a number of its important products would soon expire. For any pharmaceutical business, let alone one struggling on other counts, this would represent a deadly danger. He decided that the research department, too, had to be overhauled, and he hired Dr. Dan Azarnoff, a noted professor of pharmacology, to take it over.

Another of the problems that had been hanging over Searle was the fate of its sweetener, aspartame. After five years, not to mention the expenditure of a great deal of money, aspartame had at last been approved by the FDA in 1974. But two years later, because of the questions about Searle's research on Aldactone and Aldactazine, the FDA had decided to rescind the approval of aspartame as well. Rumsfeld regarded this decision as plainly illegitimate, and against the advice of every lawyer with whom he discussed the subject, he determined that Searle should sue the FDA. Which it did successfully in October of 1980. As a substitute for sugar in diet foods and drinks, as well as a coffee and tea sweetener under the product name Equal, aspartame began making a very substantial contribution to Searle's bottom line. And for two years in a row, 1980 and 1981, Rumsfeld was awarded the pharmaceutical industry's title of Outstanding Chief Executive Officer.

Would he have had the idea of suing the FDA if he had not himself been in the government? "I don't really know. Maybe, maybe not. When I was in Washington, particularly at the Pentagon, I had dealt with large, complicated, international enter-

prises, and now suddenly here I was, running a large, complicated international enterprise—it was a wonderful experience."

A few years later Searle was put up for sale, and in order to avoid controversy, the company withdrew its request to market a drug called gemeprost. Gemeprost was a cervical dilator, i.e., an abortifacient, an aid in, or producer of, miscarriages. (Something else the three friends decided Searle would no longer market was a line of condoms.[1])

Searle was sold in the summer of 1985. A year earlier, Rumsfeld had called all his associates together, and while informing them about the search for a buyer he announced, "We're all in this together. If it works, fine. If it doesn't work, we'll still be in this together."

Negotiations were under way with the Monsanto company. As it happened, there were actually three separate businesses involved in the sale, and at one point the Monsanto people complained that the deal was too complicated. The next morning Rumsfeld called them and said, "You're right, it's too complicated. We're calling it off." And waited coolly for Monsanto to relent, which after some months it did.

When the agreement was finally reached, it was decided between buyer and seller that the sale would be completed on a certain day just before the stock market opened and the price of the

---

[1] This product had not done very well for Searle, and indeed the company's major customer for condoms had been USAID. "Can you imagine," asked John Robson's widow, Margaret, "what the business would have lost out on with the discovery of AIDS and all those anti-teenage pregnancy campaigns?"

"When you're skiing, if you're not falling you're not trying."— Rumsfeld's Rules

stock was listed. But early on that very morning, only minutes away from the deadline, the person representing Monsanto called Rumsfeld on the phone and raised the issue of establishing a fund from which to make severance payments to those Searle employees who would be laid off. He asked Rumsfeld what he thought the amount of such a fund ought to be. Rumsfeld answered that he hadn't thought of a sum and refused to name one. The clock was ticking, but again he sat coolly by, waiting, and at the very last second, Monsanto gave in and the sale went forward as planned. The price was $2.7 billion, or $65 per share. Rumsfeld had filled the pockets of the Searles and—though it had not been, and would not ever be, a primary ambition with him—his own pockets, as well.

As might have been predicted, he now belonged to a number of corporate boards: Bendix, Sears, the Chicago Tribune, Kellogg, and others. And to the affairs of each of these companies he paid the kind of attention that many managements neither expect nor—as the corporate scandals of recent years attest—necessarily appreciate from board members. For some reason, however (perhaps someday a cultural historian will explain how and why), the men who run the major businesses in Chicago not only have certain interests in common, they also—in any case, an impressive number of them— seem to be genuine colleagues. When it comes to Chicago, the term "business community," used so freely in newspapers and magazines to denote a large and somewhat inchoate political and economic mass, is actually precise. The executives there who sit on one another's boards work together, play together, and run the civic and cultural life of the city together. Since Chicago, though a great city, is not the Garden of Eden, there must be some amount of rivalry among them. But the heat and sweat of competition, whether business or social, do not seem to reverberate down Chicago's streets and through its clubs and restaurants as they do in, say, New York. Like those houses in Winnetka, the business atmosphere of Chicago feels solid and self-confident and rich and without airs.

THE SALE of Searle would not, as it happened, mark the end of Rumsfeld's career as a Chicago businessman, but in the meantime government and politics had not entirely let go of him, either.

In the summer of 1980, for instance, as the Republicans pre-

No sport left untried

pared to nominate Ronald Reagan for president, the name of Donald Rumsfeld was on the lips of the Great Mentioner as a possible vice-presidential nominee. (This could surely not have done much to soften the old hostility of George Bush, who had been working hard—and as it would turn out, successfully—to secure that nomination for himself.)

But that he was not to be vice president did not mean that Reagan had no work for Rumsfeld to do.

In 1982, after years of negotiation, the United Nations had promulgated an agreement called the Law of the Sea Treaty, which attempted to establish international regulations governing oceanographic research as well as the mining of the seabed. Although there had been some American participation in the drawing up of this treaty, Reagan objected to it, mainly on the ground that it proposed what he believed would be a violation of American sovereignty. Reagan asked Rumsfeld if he would go on a mission to the country's allies and explain his position.

Rumsfeld then invited Kenneth Adelman, who had been with him at the Office of Economic Opportunity and had subsequently become a friend (as well as something of a playmate), to join him on the journey. In 1982, Adelman was working for Ambassador Jeane Kirkpatrick at the United Nations, and she gave him leave to go—although Rumsfeld's mission could anyway in some sense be seen as UN business. From October of 1982 to February of 1983 the two men traveled some 35,000 miles, from Paris to London to Bonn to Rome to Amsterdam, Strasbourg, Tokyo, and back to London, explaining the position of the Reagan administration and hoping to influence their hosts.[2] (During this time Rumsfeld also took the opportunity to visit a number of overseas Searle facilities.)

---

[2] Later on, Clinton would support the treaty, but it would be held up by the Senate Foreign Relations Committee.

Toward the end of that year he put himself on leave from Searle and once again took to the road at the behest of Ronald Reagan, this time as a special presidential envoy to the Middle East. During a period of thirty-seven days he visited virtually every country in the region, several of them more than once: Cypress, Saudi Arabia, Israel, Egypt, Lebanon, Jordan, Syria, Turkey, Morocco, Oman, the United Arab Emirates, Egypt, and Iraq.

Relations between Washington and Baghdad had been broken off at the time of the Six-Day War between the Arabs and Israel. But Iraq was now at war with Iran, a former friend and ally of the United States that had, with the ascension to power of the Ayatollah Khomeini, become a determined enemy. Basically, to state the proposition with a certain degree of crudity, America wanted the two countries to go on fighting without either of them emerging victorious. What followed was a policy of giving some assistance to whichever side appeared to be weakening. Iraq had originally been the aggressor in this war but was now beginning to fall behind; it would, then, need a bit of shoring up.

Thus Rumsfeld arrived in Baghdad—the highest ranking U.S. official to visit that city in six years—with a letter from Reagan to Saddam Hussein stating that Washington was preparing to resume diplomatic relations with him. (Later, according to the *New York Times,* "some American diplomats" would pronounce themselves satisfied that normal diplomatic relations had indeed been restored, at any rate in all but name.)

Shortly afterward Iran accused Iraq of using mustard gas laced with nerve agents against Iranian troops, a charge that would be confirmed by the UN and then by the United States State Department. Five years later, in 1988, it would be shown that Saddam had attacked Kurdish civilians in Iraq itself with poison gas sprayed from planes and helicopters. In response, the Senate passed a measure denying Iraq access to certain kinds of American technology. Whereupon this measure was killed by the White House. American policy, in other words, continued to be that Iraq should remain a thorn in Iran's side.

This was Ronald Reagan's policy and presumably that of at least some of his foreign and military advisers. But was it Rumsfeld's? Again, as with all policies of a president he happens to be serving, he will not say—though it certainly does not fit with any of his known habits of thinking about the world and America's role in it. But the envoy carrying Reagan's message to Saddam Hussein in 1983 remained true to the man man who, as Ford's chief of staff, had declared it essential to bear in mind that the Constitution provides for only one president at a time. (This was one of the early principles set down in the document known as "Rumsfeld's Rules"—his now famous collection of observations about life in general and Washington in particular. "Don't begin to think you're the president. You're not. The Constitution provides for only one," is a rule that figures early and prominently on the list. The one that follows is, "In the execution of presidential decisions work to be true to his views, in fact and tone."

Rumsfeld had one other haunting task to perform as Middle East envoy, and that was to inform Amin Gemayel, the ill-starred leader of the once beautiful and soon to be godforsaken country of Lebanon, that the United States was pulling out the marines we had sent to Beirut. This was a move long argued over, one that had given rise to a disagreement between the State Department and the Pentagon.

The marines had been sent to help keep the peace in an ugly civil war that had for some time been pitting Lebanese Christians against Lebanese Muslims. This struggle had been further complicated by the presence in Lebanon of Palestinian refugees living under the authority of the Palestine Liberation Organization and who had among other things committed atrocities on certain Christian villages. In 1982, the Israel army invaded Lebanon, at first for the purpose of putting an end to the bombardment of Israel's northern cities, and then moving northward all the way to Beirut in hot pursuit of the PLO. The United States determined that the PLO "fighters" should be rescued and assigned the marines to provide them with safe passage to Tunis. After seeing Arafat and his minions safely ensconced in North Africa, the marines were ordered to return to Lebanon and resume their efforts as peacekeepers (over the most strenuous objections of Secretary of Defense Caspar Weinberger).

Then on April 18, 1983, the U.S. Embassy in Beirut was hit by a terrorist bomb that left 63 dead and 120 wounded; and finally, on October 23 a 12,000-pound bomb destroyed the Marine Corps barracks in Beirut, killing 241 marines and seriously wounding 80 others. These two events precipitated a great debate within the U.S. government, a debate that ended with the decision to remove U.S. forces. It was Rumsfeld's duty to inform Gemayel of this decision, which would, in relatively short order, amount to the death knell of the Gemayel government and ultimately of Lebanese sovereignty itself. A sad errand indeed.

A FTER RETURNING from this mission Rumsfeld embarked on a new adventure from which he would, once again, learn much—though not exactly what he had hoped to learn.

What happened was that some time in late 1985 rumors began to circulate around Washington that Donald Rumsfeld was thinking of getting into the presidential race. When questioned about it, the *Washington Post* said, "he does not demur." Though exploring a presidential candidacy would set him on another collision course with now Vice President George H. W. Bush[3]—and though he was coming in last in the opinion polls—it was after all still early days.

Rumsfeld spent much of 1987 traveling around the country making speeches; in roughly a year's time he visited 185 cities in more than 30 states. If in the end his support proved to be thin on the ground, he was not without distinguished advocates. A column by George Will, for instance, speculated that "this former naval aviator (he taught formation flying: *Top Gun* for president?) and collegiate wrestling champion has a flintiness, a hardness in his gaze and temperament, that could make him a serious contender in the 1988 race to replace Ronald Reagan as Republican heartthrob."

"Flintiness" and "hardness" were not qualities ever associated with the heartthrob capacity of Ronald Reagan—quite the opposite. Nor would Rumsfeld's friends have singled these out as his leading traits. (*Top Gun,* on the other hand, would undoubtedly have been found quite acceptable.) But in couching his approval in this way, Will was more than anything else expressing the hope, a hope shared in those days by many of Will's conservative companions-in-arms, that when Ronald Reagan left the White House the United States would not once again commence to wilt as it had in the days of Carter.

But with his name never moving up from last place in the polls, Rumsfeld announced on April 2, 1987, that he was no longer a candidate. In any case, the fix for Bush was surely in, as it seems to have been from the moment of Reagan's reelection in 1984. (Which, incidentally, did not prevent Rumsfeld from cementing an

---

[3] In the period since World War II, it seems to have become almost an article of political faith that the vice president is somehow the rightful heir of his party's candidacy for president.

old enmity by backing Dole for the nomination and going to New Hampshire on his behalf once he himself was out of the race.)

Why had he run? To be sure, around and behind every candidate for public office, and especially every candidate for the presidency, there are friends and admirers and well-wishers, along with the inevitable would-be exploiters, urging him to become a candidate and presenting him with arguments for why he must inevitably win. Moreover, for the first time in his life Donald Rumsfeld now had some real money in the bank and happened to be out of a job. That he, as always, had energy to burn goes without saying. Still, he had chosen to go for the great brass ring from a spot that was not even on the carousel. Which is to say, he had for a number of years been out of the public eye. Even before that, he had for some time been in it only by occupying the kind of position—such as White House chief of staff—that does not yield up much, if indeed any, political gold. Around this time he himself told an interviewer that the most difficult transition for him had been the change from being an elected representative to becoming a White House official, and that moving from there into business had been much easier. But the leap back into electoral politics turned out to be a bigger one than he had supposed.

While he was traveling around testing the presidential waters, however, something that would in the long run be of far greater consequence to his life had come to preoccupy him. For in addition to selling his candidacy he was also attempting to stir up interest in an issue that in those days was viewed by most voters as quite remote from their everyday concerns. That issue was Middle Eastern terrorism.

After September 11, 2001, it may be difficult to believe, but in the late eighties, except to certain specialists in the field, an invitation to be concerned with the problem of terrorism seemed a bit odd and maybe even cranky.

It was not that Americans had been completely untouched by this problem. There had, for instance, been an outpouring of public horror and anger over the bombing of the marine barracks in Lebanon; the subsequent hijacking of the ship *Achille Lauro* by Palestinian terrorists, in the course of which an American consigned to a wheelchair was thrown overboard to his death, had also occasioned a good many expressions of public outrage. But like the terrorists themselves, terrorism continued to be viewed by most Americans as something exotic, belonging to far-off places and unfamiliar peoples. (Even the first, happily not too successful, bombing of the World Trade Center in 1993 would fail to ignite the kind of fear that might only eight years later have been useful to those in charge of keeping their fellow citizens safe.)

Be that as it may, soon after the *Achille Lauro* incident, Rumsfeld gave a speech in Albuquerque, New Mexico (a place not unacquainted with crime but in those days one in which an ordinary citizen might have imagined that Middle Eastern terrorists were men from Mars). In that speech he pointed out that terrorism was not merely a matter of random incidents perpetrated by groups of unhappy people but was actually nothing less than outright warfare. Moreover, he warned, it was a kind of warfare that the United States had better immediately take steps to deter.

There is no record of how the Albuquerque audience responded to this formulation, though the evidence of subsequent history would suggest that it was on the whole lethargic.

But there was nothing lethargic about Rumsfeld's pursuit of the issue. Over and over again, and in terms that nowadays seem veritably prophetic, he insisted both on the danger of terrorism and on the need for policies to counter it. One policy he emphasized was for the United States to go after the terrorists on their own home ground rather than wait until we needed to be protected on ours. Another was to recognize that the United States cannot really deter terrorism in the Middle East "until it redefines the process as warfare by hostile governments rather than isolated acts."

Such prescience about the state of the world, as rare in those days as it would turn out to have been urgently needed, was of little help to a would-be candidate for the 1988 presidential nomination. Those members of the Ford administration who had charged Rumsfeld with being a ruthless, if brilliant, self-serving bureaucrat—such as the old quartet of Kissinger, Rockefeller, Simon, and Bush *père*—would have had reason to wonder how, if it were not out of a higher concern for the safety and well-being of his country, he could have blundered so badly in finding a message.

Meanwhile, back in Illinois, rumors of his candidacy for other offices were constantly being floated, whether in an upcoming race for the senate or a subsequent one for the governorship. "It seemed to Valerie and me at that point," said his daughter Marcy, "that every year he was rumored to be the leading candidate for something."

In the end, he would not run for anything again. Had he, then, lost his taste for electoral office, or was there now perhaps only one such office that could satisfy it—and that one unreachable?

I N EARLY May of 1988, Rumsfeld's mother died. Throughout her husband's last years, during which, afflicted with Alzheimer's, he may not even have known who she was, she remained as attentive to him and his needs as she had been during his years in the navy. Nor did she ever cease believing that she could find the way to spark some awareness of his surroundings in him; sometimes she would take him driving to an old haunt, hoping in vain that he would respond to it. Her granddaughter Marcy says of her, "She was lively and sharp. She liked thinking and she liked ideas. And above all, she loved to laugh." She had reached her eighty-fourth year; she had seen her two children well and happily married and had watched them prosper in the world. And she had seen her son find ever new prestigious outlets for his driving energy. Even her anxieties about his taking over Searle had turned out to be bootless. She had been hurt in an automobile accident but had recovered, or so the doctors believed. But she hadn't, and slowly grew weaker until one day she was gone.

I N SEPTEMBER, with Bush *père*'s presidential campaign now in full swing (a situation in which many an old wound is temporarily forgotten), Don joined the task force advising the candidate on national security issues—along with Kissinger, Zbigniew Bzezinski, Al Haig, and others. And a bit later the ever-active Chicago rumor mill began buzzing with the highly improbable idea that he was being considered for a position in George Bush's cabinet.[4]

Someone who was actually named to that cabinet, however—as secretary of defense—was John Tower, one of the Senate's staunchest advocates of American military power. But Tower's hearings before the Senate Armed Services Committee (a committee on which he himself had formerly served as chairman) were given over to a goodly amount of nasty testimony replete with gos-

---

[4] Indeed, far from offering him a Cabinet job, Bush had even nixed his appointment to serve as the chairman of a new advisory committee for the Food and Drug Administration set up to investigate the unfair pricing of generic drugs.

The farm

sip about his weakness—previously unheard of in Washington, of course—for alcohol and ladies not his wife. Senator John Glenn even went so far as to read from confidential documents produced by the FBI's investigation of Tower. Not surprisingly, given the onslaught on his character, Tower's nomination was voted down in committee without being sent to the Senate floor.

Bush's next nominee for defense was one that gladdened Rumsfeld's heart: his former deputy and dear friend Dick Cheney. Still, he sent a letter to William Sessions, then director of the FBI, announcing that he would from henceforth no longer cooperate

with the FBI in its checking of the backgrounds of top-level White House nominees. "Unverified information received in the course of FBI background checks," he wrote with Tower in mind, "was made available to members of the U.S. Senate by the executive branch of government," and he did not wish to be "a part of or contribute to a process that works in this manner."

Rumsfeld had nothing to gain from this gesture, of course, neither for himself nor for his friend Dick Cheney, and one would probably not go too far wrong in supposing that neither William Sessions nor the Chairman of the Senate Armed Services Committee had ever received any other letter like it.

The farmer

5

THE WILD BLUE YONDER

H E WAS fifty-eight years old and still, as they say, full of beans. The question was, what was he to do now? The answer would not be long in coming. Among his several corporate board memberships (to which new ones, it seemed, were being added month by month) was that of the investment firm of Forstmann Little. Now, in August of 1990 Forstmann Little happened to acquire a company called General Instruments that was headquartered in New York City. GI was the country's largest manufacturer of cable boxes for television sets and had joined in a race against the Japanese to produce high-definition television (a race, by the way, which it would win). Like Searle, GI had over the years acquired a number of businesses that bore some kind of rough relation to one another. But,

Time out: the Rumsfelds in Taos, New Mexico

again like Searle in 1977, the company was clearly in need of some Rumsfeld-style corporate ministration. Accordingly, in October of 1990, Forstmann Little announced that Donald Rumsfeld had been appointed GI's chairman and CEO.

The first thing he set out to do, as might have been expected, was apply his now well-honed corporate knife. In four weeks he managed to reduce the company's management staff from 160 to 60. Before long, he also sold off one of the businesses that was un-related to the company's main interests—Defense Systems Group, manufacturers of radar systems for fighter aircraft.

During the following April he moved GI's headquarters to Chicago, the city in which he had not only decided he would con-tinue to live (while commuting back and forth to New York) but in which he much preferred to conduct business. ("Chicago's distinc-tiveness," he told the *Chicago Tribune,* "is in being a real commu-nity . . . the essence of which is diversity.")

After two years of Rumsfeld's chairmanship, with sales up from $234 million to $298 million, the company at last posted a fourth quarter profit. A few months later, Rumsfeld announced that while he would remain on the company's board, he was retir-ing as CEO. He had been running GI for three years, adding hand-somely to Forstmann Little's coffers and to his own financial condition, as well. If this could not quite be accounted compensa-tion for his failure to become a viable candidate for the presidency, it at least added a good deal both to his own sense of, as well as his reputation for, being someone whose future was still very much before him.

Down through the years Rumsfeld had been spending a good deal of time and energy serving not only on numerous corporate boards but also on the boards of certain nonprofit institutions de-voted in one way or another to public affairs—particularly foreign and defense policy—such as the RAND Corporation, the Hoover

Institution, the Institute for Contemporary Affairs, and the Committee for the Free World. And during the 1990s, especially after he stopped running General Instruments, board memberships of both kinds grew almost exponentially. All these memberships left him with little time on his hands. For one thing, they involved an almost dizzying amount of travel; and for another, the enterprises he was required to think about and help provide for—from electrical engineering to biotech to breakfast cereal to teaching economics to rescuing refugees, and, as always, to foreign and military affairs—were varied enough to require both a good deal of physical effort and a constantly replenished supply of intellectual energy. It was a situation that came very close to his idea, as he once put it to an interviewer, of "living each year and enjoying the heck out of it."

If this was his notion of enjoyment, he would soon be in for another large dose of it. In January of 1998 Congress appointed a commission to assess the nature and the extent of the emerging threat to the United States from ballistic missiles, and Rumsfeld was appointed its chairman. For the rest, the commission consisted of eight other men of distinction—two retired air force generals, a former director of the CIA, a former member of the president's Science Advisory Committee, a deputy administrator of NASA, a former undersecretary of defense for policy, a former undersecretary of state for security, and a former assistant director of the U.S. Arms Control and Disarmament Agency. (The former undersecretary of defense for policy, Paul Wolfowitz, would become Rumsfeld's deputy during his second tour at the Pentagon.) They were given six months to submit a report of their findings.

The issue of how to think about, and what to do about, America's vulnerability to Soviet ballistic missiles had been around as long as the missiles themselves. As far as the general public was concerned, there were periods when missiles had been the subject of a good deal of passionate debate. There were other times, however—either because the threat was too frightening or because an attack on the United States seemed too improbable—when the issue appeared to have flown quite out of the public mind.

President Ronald Reagan had, of course, been subjected to a goodly amount of noisy ridicule and no less noisy moral attack for expressing his belief that the United States could, and should, undertake to create and deploy some kind of defensive system for destroying incoming missiles in flight. As a token of its supposed space-fantasy quality, Reagan's proposal had been dubbed "Star Wars." But since there had not yet been any clinching technological success with any of the various systems then being tested, the whole issue was for a time quite easily brushed aside by the opponents of missile defense. They argued, first, that the very idea was pie-in-the-sky and could never work, and that, in any case, it was essential for the country to *remain* undefended against Soviet missiles. According to the theory behind the policy known, through a stroke of conscious or unconscious genius, as "MAD" (or Mutual Assured Destruction), nuclear war between the United States and the Soviet Union could best be prevented if both countries' populations were to be kept vulnerable to attack. It followed that building a defense against attack would be provocative and destabilizing. Worse yet, in the view of some, the feeling of perfect security might tempt the United States to engage in reckless and aggressive foreign adventures.

Aside from the people openly hostile to missile defense on these grounds, there were those with an abiding faith in diplomacy who believed that the United States would sooner or later be able to negotiate missiles out of existence. Others, perhaps of a more cynical turn of mind, had an abiding faith in money and thought that missiles in unfriendly places could be bribed away with Yankee dollars. And finally for still others, the collapse of the Soviet

Union, followed by an ostensible warming in U.S.-Russian relations, seemed to have taken a good deal of the sting out of the problem—or to have relegated it to some spot farther down on the list of popular anxieties.

But it could not for long be ignored by the United States government that there were a number of hostile or potentially hostile nations, most particularly in Asia and the Middle East, who—beyond the reach of treaties and/or bribes—were either developing ballistic missiles for themselves or acquiring them from others. Such nations most prominently included China, North Korea, Iran, Iraq, Pakistan, and India. Of course, there was still Russia (as that country would once again be called) to think about. Hence the appointment of a "Commission to Assess the Ballistic Missile Threat to the United States."

The questions that the commission put to itself were basically two: First, just how widely was missile technology actually being disseminated, and second, given the United States' own technological superiority in this field, just how great a danger to us was there from the missile programs of the less advanced nations? What, for instance, would it take, both in terms of time and in the way of technological advancement, for such missiles to be armed with weapons of mass destruction, and how many years would it take for at least some of these countries to develop missiles that might even reach the United States?

Thus the commission set out to assess the threat from missiles that were being deployed on the territory of a hostile or potentially hostile country, missiles that might be launched from aircraft or from a surface vessel or submarine off the coasts of the United States, and missiles emplaced by a potentially hostile nation on the territory of a third country in order to bring them within striking distance of the United States.

A question the commission did not deal with directly was what impact these missiles could or would have on U.S. military strategy. Though its official report does mention how much difficulty the United States had in trying to deal with Iraq's Scuds during the Gulf War, the military/political issue of what to do about such missiles was deliberately set aside. For the thinking was that the essential task was to arrive at an estimate of where missiles were being produced and just how advanced the technology involved in producing them might be.

Not surprisingly, the Rumsfeld commission found nothing at all with which to cheer the members of the House or Senate who might have been hoping to be reassured. Even the fact that North Korea's or Pakistan's or Iraq's missiles were less reliable than those of the United States—which, of course, they were—did not mean that they were not mortally dangerous. Indeed, the commission found, it was possible that they might be upgraded as early as within the next five years. In addition, if things were to continue as they had been going, these missiles could be upgraded virtually out of earshot of the American intelligence community. And while it seemed less and less likely that the Russians would actually launch an attack against the United States, Russia continued to pose a threat as a major exporter of ballistic missile technology to others. As did China.

One of the problems faced by the commission and its chairman, and rather sternly alluded to in its report, was the inadequacy of American intelligence. This inadequacy was all the more troubling for being less technical than intellectual. According to Rumsfeld and company, the usual practice of intelligence gatherers was to try to measure how far some country's ballistic missile program had progressed beyond its starting point, whereas what really needed to be determined was how close a particular country might have come to being capable of launching a long-range missile.

When programs were assessed in terms of what was concretely

known about them, the commission found the assessments tended to lag behind what was actually going on by from two to eight years (and sometimes completely missed what had been going on). Or, in a formulation that could only have come from the pen of the commission's chairman himself, "A narrow focus on the certain obscures the almost-certain."

The commission's report thus provided a country by country estimate of missile capability. North Korea, for example, was said to have a medium-range missile and was working hard to develop a longer-range one (while also maintaining an active program of producing weapons of mass destruction—WMDs—including the ability to deploy chemical, biological, and nuclear-armed warheads). India, which also had biological- and chemical-weapons programs, and which had detonated a nuclear device as long ago as 1974, was developing a variety of missiles, particularly with the help of the Russians but also with some help from Western Europe and the United States. Pakistan, with assistance from the Chinese, had been able to build a ballistic-missile infrastructure that was by then more advanced than that of North Korea. And so on.

Some of the countries surveyed had refused to sign any agreements committing them to nonproliferation. Some had signed such agreements and then cheated. In any case, the commission found, the steady increase in global trade had made possible a corresponding increase in the availability of information, technology, and technicians—and with these, the spread of WMDs along with the means for delivering them over greater and greater distances. A threat to the United States from ballistic missiles armed with weapons of mass destruction was therefore not likely to be far off.

(One country about which Rumsfeld was, and would remain, particularly concerned was China. "An awful lot of Chinese military doctrine," he says, "talks about leapfrogging generations of capabilities and moving toward threats to the United States." Once in the Pentagon, he would advocate putting an end to all military contacts with Beijing, but would be overruled by the National Security Council, especially by Secretary of State Colin Powell, who continues to favor friendly engagement with the Chinese. And not long after this disagreement, both Rumsfeld and Bush would become enmeshed in a particular aspect of the threat the ballistic-missile commission had earlier laid out. Indeed, had Rumsfeld known how soon life would require him to focus on the threat from North Korean missiles, he would have looked at the commission's work with an even greater measure of concern, if not, indeed, alarm.)

The report concludes with a discussion of what is known in the world of military acronyms as RMA, or "Revolution in Military Affairs." Key to this revolution are precision-guided munitions, stealth technology, and space-based equipment for command and control, communications, surveillance, and reconnaissance—along with the computer-based capacity to make these capabilities work together. The objective of RMA, the report points out—in a summary that, again, will echo fatefully for the commission's chairman some four years down the road—is to make United States forces "lighter but more lethal, so that fewer personnel with less equipment can strike over longer distances and with a far more powerful effect."

Whether Congress meant to do anything with these findings was unclear. The man who had been responsible for creating the commission, Speaker of the House Newt Gingrich, resigned under a cloud only four months after the commission's report was submitted.

But once again, as he had some years before on the issue of terrorism, Rumsfeld took to the hustings to warn about the need for the country to defend itself against an ever growing missile threat. And this time it began to enter the consciousness of a growing number of people that some very unpleasant and unfriendly nations were doing such unpleasant and unfriendly things as producing, exporting, and upgrading ballistic missiles that might, before too many decades had gone by, reach the United States. At least some of the people whose consciousness was being raised in this way, moreover, would soon take over the government and exercise more than a little influence over their country's future.

T HIS WOULD not quite be the case, however, with the next commission Rumsfeld was asked to chair: the Commission to Assess United States National Security Space Management and Organization. For while space is for the most part an entertaining and even sometimes thrilling subject for Americans, especially young ones, to contemplate (as well as to watch movies about), the combination of space with national security is something about which many people continue to feel nervous. If Ronald Reagan was greeted with ridicule, others have been downright reviled for believing in the possibility of a space-based defense against enemy missiles. To some extent, this opposition grew out of the theory behind the policy of Mutually Assured Destruction. But when it finally became undeniable that the Soviets were not keeping to the terms of MAD, the argument against missile defense shifted from security to viability. Most recently, in the face of a convincing body of evidence that it was by now not only possible but in fact perfectly feasible to build a space-based missile defense, the opposition seemed to move into the realm of the purely emotional, where thinking was simply shut down.

This second commission, too, was given six months in which to prepare a report. It was set a somewhat more various, if to the commissioners perhaps a less worrying, task than had been set for the ballistic-missile commission: to recommend what should be done about organizing, or if necessary reorganizing, the military services in order to enhance their operations through the use of assets in space.

The commission met more than thirty times and was briefed by experts in both intelligence and military affairs. Not surprisingly, a number of difficulties and shortcomings in the then-current management of space were found. Among these difficulties and shortcomings was the fact that while each branch of the military had been directed to execute space programs and integrate space into its strategy and training, there was no single service whose full responsibility it was to "organize, train, and equip" for space. And though the air force had been given most of the budget for space activity, many of the experts advising the commission doubted that the air force was up to the job of providing the technology for both the use and defense of space by the other branches of the military. The commissioners also found that the National Reconnaissance Office, which had started out as a small and agile organization originally put together to meet the U.S. government's needs for space-borne reconnaissance, had grown from being a leader in the development of first-of-a-kind systems into the somewhat bogged-down manager of the systems it had already developed.

Another problem concerned the staff within the CIA responsible for managing resources and assessing space programs: It lacked the authority and the flexibility to use its budget in a way that genuinely reflected its needs. Furthermore, in thinking about the problems connected with the budgeting process, the commission found that the authorization and appropriation of funding for space routinely involved at least six congressional committees, each of which tended to mirror the particular interests it was given the task of overseeing. The result was that officials of the executive

branch were forced to spend—or waste—a great deal of time and energy trying to work with a large number of committees and sub-committees with overlapping jurisdictions. A final point was that as high-tech weapons continued to spread through the world market, it would be increasingly difficult for the United States to maintain its technological superiority.

The commission offered a variety of recommendations for dealing with these problems, such as reorganizing and reassigning authority within the Department of Defense in order both to integrate present space technologies and acquire new ones. It further recommended incorporating the country's civil and commercial space activities within the national security space services, setting up a more rational and efficient system of budgeting, and modernizing war games and simulations of war-fighting to include the capabilities of space systems.

Through it all, Rumsfeld kept a tight and smooth hand over the proceedings, so that despite many differences of opinion among its members (not to mention among the experts who served as consultants), the commission managed to produce a final report without any minority objections. No small feat for a group whose members represented such a variety of backgrounds, positions, and inclinations and each of whom could claim a goodly amount of authority in his own field.

QUITE APART from the weight of the issues they engaged, what is striking about the deliberations of these commissions—both the one investigating the proliferation of ballistic missiles and the one assessing the condition of the various security-based space programs—is the fun they also gave rise to. Perhaps exchanges of wit are a not uncommon form of relief for people

engaged in contemplating frightening or dreary or even just arcane problems. Still, neither of these subjects might have been considered much of an inspiration for flights of high spirits or humor. But to think so is to reckon without the presence of Donald Rumsfeld.

Rumsfeld had, of course, already acquired a good deal of fame (and would in the rather near future acquire a good deal more) as the author-collector of that seemingly ever-ongoing collection of apothegms and aphorisms called "Rumsfeld's Rules." That the compiler of these "rules" was someone who refused to remain conventionally dour in the face of problems and circumstances of the highest seriousness would one day become evident to the whole world. Meanwhile, the sometimes merely clever, and sometimes profoundly clever, exchanges that lightened the hours spent by the commissioners at their less than frolicsome task were faithfully recorded by the chairman—along with a number of apposite remarks made by historical figures and a number of pithy observations that were recognizable from their style as Rumsfeld's own. He called this collection, after one of the proposed techniques for missile defense, "Brilliant Pebbles." Indeed, one member of the space commission confessed that as a result of Rumsfeld's habit of recording their witticisms, by the end they had all begun to rack their brains to find clever or amusing ways of saying what they wanted to say.

A few examples of these Brilliant Pebbles will give their flavor—along with something of the atmosphere of the proceedings:

- "The worst mistake is to have the best ladder and the wrong wall."

At home on the range

- "Nothing ages so quickly as yesterday's vision of the future."
- "We'll fix the enemy; we'll leak our acquisition system to them."
- "One thing we've learned about tsars is that the barons ignore them and the peasants kill them."
- "The U.S. Air Force is tribal: if you leave the campground, they burn your teepee and shoot your pony."
- "Government does two things well—nothing and overreact."
- "A friend in Washington, D.C., is someone who stabs you in the chest."

Rumsfeld was required to resign from the space management commission on December 28, 2000, two weeks before it was due to shut down. For that was the day on which he was nominated by President-elect George W. Bush to serve for the second time as secretary of defense. Perhaps, then—in a turn of events that was unusual for the ordinary run of such commissions—the findings of the two he had chaired would soon be taken with the utmost seriousness, if not in Congress then at least within certain high reaches of the Pentagon.

MANY YEARS earlier, while he was still the CEO of Searle, Rumsfeld had told an interviewer that he always imagined he would return to Washington some day. He very much enjoyed being a businessman, he said, but he had also enjoyed being in government and thought that he had been good at it: He had, after all, invested many years of his life in becoming good at it.

But if in early January 2001 he was fully prepared to return to his earlier haunts—indeed, to the very job he had left twenty-four years earlier—Joyce Rumsfeld was not, at least not yet, ready for the change. "There I was," she said, "imagining without thinking it through that I would somehow go on living in Chicago and commute to Washington. Then one day I found myself in a Senate chamber attending Don's confirmation hearing. I sat there listening, and at some point in the proceedings it was as if a big curtain had suddenly been pulled aside in my head. Oh, I thought, I remember this—I remember now what this is like. It's real. It's full time. It's nothing for dabbling around in."

So once again, as on occasions almost beyond numbering in the preceding forty-five years, she would set about finding and organizing a new home. It seems safe to say, however, that curtains opening or not, neither of the Rumsfelds on that day could have begun to imagine what the future held in store for them.

6

BACK IN THE
SADDLE AGAIN

DECEMBER 28 was very late for the appointment of a secretary of defense. There would now be less than a month for the new nominee to do much serious planning for how to take over and manage an enterprise that may in its way be more messy and complicated than any in Washington.

To begin with, the office of the secretary of defense is planted at the very heart of a vast sprawl of needs and urgencies and competing demands that make up both the daily diet and the underlying culture of the United States military establishment. Moreover, the office is set in this competitive sprawl literally as well as figuratively. For the secretary sits not in one of those stately historic

Bush and Rumsfeld: rethinking America's doctrine

structures, touched by the hopes and graces of a long and splendid past, that are arrayed across the Potomac River in the District of Columbia. Rather his office is in that massive, modern, hulking edifice called the Pentagon.

The Pentagon is an almost perfect architectural expression of the haste and sense of emergency with which it was originally built. It had been planned to provide office space to accommodate some 40,000 people who by 1941 were then scattered among seventeen different government buildings in the District of Columbia. These were the employees of the mushrooming World War II military establishment. The plan for this monumental establishment is said to have been drawn up in the space of something like *four days* during the summer of 1941 and the building to have opened for business in less than a year and a half after that.

In its own literature the Pentagon boasts that it is the world's most efficient office building. Whether that is or is not the case, it is also very much a bricks-and-mortar expression of the peculiar ambivalence—trust/unease—with which the country has continued to view what goes on inside. For surely no great world power in history has ever maintained so strictly utilitarian and homely a monument to its military might—vast without being imposing and modern without a justifying modern aesthetic. (During the days of demonstrations against the Vietnam War a group of sixties protesters announced that they planned to form a circle around the building and levitate it with chanting, which was after all a curiously intimate thing for them to have thought of doing. They were not serious, of course, these demonstrators, but whatever else can be said about them, this plan of theirs surely gave no evidence that they felt themselves to be coming up against a symbol of the world's most overwhelming aggregation of power.)

In returning to the Pentagon Rumsfeld was returning to a place whose difficulties and discomforts had once been familiar to him.

But after a quarter of a century the world was a different world, the threats to the security of the United States were different threats, and the faces and attitudes in the building were bound in some telling measure to be different faces and attitudes.

On the other hand, while the military were no longer sunk in the post-Vietnam atmosphere of failure and depression of the 1970s and had long since come to be at ease about presiding over an all-volunteer force, they were still very far from being in as vibrant and feisty a condition as their twenty-first secretary.

One of the reasons for this was that little by little over the years, and to a truly marked degree during the Clinton administration, Congress had in effect replaced the executive branch in the job of looking after the Pentagon. There were now hundreds of people working in the building whose only role was to serve members of Congress: answering their inquiries, tending to their interests, and doing them favors. And the favors done for congressmen were only too duly reciprocated: It seemed that virtually every special budgetary request, along with every new weapons system, not to speak of many a no-longer-needed military base, had its advocates in the House and Senate. An inevitable—and for Rumsfeld a most trying—corollary was that there were now many members of Congress who expected that he, too, along with his new appointees, would be offering them his full attention.

The way of life of the Pentagon had also been very much influenced by the fact that, again most particularly during the Clinton administration, a number of appointees in the Department of Defense had themselves once been members of Congress. Legislators being people who are—and who are in the nature of things required to be—dependent for their effectiveness on the building of consensus, they tend to be more forgiving of one another's weaknesses than would, say, most business executives. The result was a notable falling off of something essential to both the makers of war and the keepers of peace: a willingness to give an accounting of oneself.

Aside from the sheer organizational difficulties created in such an atmosphere, the serious abdication of authority over the military by Bill Clinton (and inevitably, therefore, also of the secretaries of defense who had served under him) led to certain other problems. It had, for one thing, become virtually impossible to keep any military secrets: Legislators who had the run of the Pentagon also often had friendly—and information-hungry—contacts in the press.

Then, too, without civilian control the military, especially the staff of the joint chiefs, inevitably became the managers of their own affairs. This came more and more to mean that military promotions were determined on the basis not of ability but of congeniality with one's fellows. And this in turn meant that some of the most capable people, discouraged in such an atmosphere about what a future with the armed forces might hold for them, were leaving the military for greener pastures.

This was the situation into which Rumsfeld now entered. In the course of his discussions with the president-elect, and subsequently the newly inaugurated president, he discovered that the two of them were in complete agreement about their priorities with respect to the Pentagon. In the course of his campaign Bush had declared his intention to remake the American military, which was, he said, still operating on the basis of its experience in the century now past—indeed, operating on the basis of a doctrine that had remained virtually unchanged since the Kennedy administration. That was when Robert S. McNamara, Kennedy's secretary of defense, had adopted the "two and a half wars" policy, under which the United States should be capable of fighting two major wars simultaneously, one against the Soviets in Europe and one, say, against the Chinese in Asia, along with a minor war somewhere else. And though the armed forces were never actually provided with either the level of equipment or preparedness to follow through on this policy if called upon to do so, the doctrine behind it had essentially never been rethought. (In Nixon's time the number of major wars had been cut from two to one, and the policy had thereby, in theory at least, come somewhat closer to the country's actual level of capability.)

Under these circumstances, Bush and Rumsfeld agreed—to what would be the dismay of the Pentagon brass—not to request any increase in the military budget, at least not until the new secretary had completed a full-scale assessment of the country's military doctrine. In addition to military doctrine, Rumsfeld would also be required to undertake a top-to-bottom review of the current state of the country's military capabilities.[1]

I N JUNE of 2001, testifying before the Senate Armed Services Committee, he argued that a new military strategy had to be developed. In the course of his presentation, he spoke about the need to be prepared for unforeseen threats. "The only thing we know for certain," he said, "is that it is unlikely that any of us knows what is likely." He then went on to list the kinds of blindness to the future that had become manifest just in his own lifetime. For instance, he pointed out, during the Depression the assumption behind defense planning had been "no war for ten years." The fleet that was to be the great deterrent to war became the first target of war in 1941, whereas aircraft that had not even existed at the beginning of the century became critical to the outcome of World

---

[1] Some part of which, of course, he had already begun to do with the commissions on ballistic missiles and space defense.

War II. Then with the atomic age, the Soviet Union, our recent ally, became our main adversary. In the early sixties few people were paying attention to a country called Vietnam, but by the end of the decade the United States was embroiled in a very costly war there. In the mid seventies Iran was a key U.S. ally, but only a few years later it would be transformed by a ferociously anti-Western revolution. Finally, in March 1989, when the current vice president, Dick Cheney, appeared before the Senate to be confirmed as secretary of defense, not one person uttered the word *Iraq,* and yet within a year Cheney would be preparing for the Gulf War. It was time, then, Rumsfeld concluded, for a new doctrine that would allow us enough flexibility to meet the new uncertainties up ahead.

On hearing this analysis, the legislators may have nodded piously, but as for the military themselves, a review of both their theories of warfare and their organizational behavior—let alone the demand that they begin thinking about uncertainties and unknowables—was far from what they had been expecting of the new administration. This was particularly so in view of the powerful roles to be played in this administration by not merely one but two men who had once, so to speak, been their own: not only Donald Rumsfeld but the new vice president, as well.

So on top of their very bitter disappointment at the discovery that Rumsfeld was to be no automatic champion of budget increases, many of them were deeply disturbed by his determination to examine their doctrine and to review their capabilities. From the point of view of many who would be required to participate in it or pay special attention to it, such a review promised to involve a potentially serious disruption of their accustomed rounds. But above all, some members of the military would later tell interviewers, they feared that the future of the institution to which they had devoted their lives was being shaped without seriously consulting them. And indeed, even without going through the process of a review, Rumsfeld undoubtedly had in mind a good deal—in the view of Richard Perle, then chairman of the Defense Policy Board, a group of knowledgeable laymen who met with and advised the secretary from time to time, at least 80 percent—of what would need to be done.[2]

Rumsfeld's difficulties actually began on January 27, the very first morning after his swearing in, when the *National Journal* reported that the military planners were working night and day to prepare their wish lists for new hardware. They were confident, it was reported, that Bush and Cheney and Rumsfeld would very soon be asking Congress to raise the defense budget for fiscal 2002 to a sum way above the $310 billion that Clinton had proposed for it. Here, then, within as little as twenty-four hours, was the opening round of what was to become an ongoing struggle.

Next, there was the problem of the staff of the joint chiefs of staff, whose members had grown accustomed to governing themselves and who were consequently resisting the new secretary's efforts to assume control of the department. It would take a number of months and much tension and unhappiness to sort out the distribution of authority between them. The Constitution, Rumsfeld would remark over and over, provides for—indeed *requires*—civilian control of the military, but this fundamental principle of American governance seemed in recent years to have gone considerably by the board.

"The first thing you have to do," he would later tell *Fortune,* "is be willing to set priorities. Once you do that, you have said that something is more important than something else, and somebody is not going to like it. And that's life."

---

[2] When this was repeated to him, he said nothing but merely grinned from ear to ear.

On top of the resistance he was encountering in and from the Pentagon, the Senate was proving recalcitrant about confirming Rumsfeld's appointments. He and his deputy secretary, Paul Wolfowitz, found themselves virtually alone in that enormous institution until the month of June, and even then the process was incomplete: Rumsfeld had forty-three positions to fill, and some of them were delayed until as late as midsummer. One of the major obstacles to the hiring process was said to have originated in the office of Trent Lott, who was allegedly taking this way of showing his annoyance at the secretary for not being sufficiently attentive to him. But whether the difficulty mainly lay with Lott or was, as seems likely, more widely shared among various other barons of the Senate, it took a very long time for the new secretary to get even a minimal staff up and running.

Ken and Carol Adelman had introduced him to Wolfowitz many years earlier, when Rumsfeld asked them to arrange an evening of interesting conversation: not many conversations are more interesting than those with Paul Wolfowitz, a former mathematician, a sometime academic, and someone with years of experience as a diplomat as well as a policy planner in the Defense Department. After that the two men were engaged in a couple of projects together—such as a commission on Japan headed by George Shultz and, of course, the commission on ballistic missiles. On learning of Rumsfeld's appointment, Wolfowitz, who had come to admire him enormously, immediately applied for the post of deputy secretary, and after a bit of suspense was given the job.

Anyone familiar with the Rumsfeldian management style at Searle and General Instruments might have expected that Rumsfeld would deal with the staff of the joint chiefs quickly and from strength rather than attempt to arrive at some kind of workable arrangement with them. But the military is a rather different animal from a body of corporate employees, having as it does its own traditions and sources of authority. In addition, there had been a great deal beyond the Pentagon proper for Rumsfeld to deal with. During his first six months he also needed to spend a goodly amount of time at the White House, getting to know his president and discussing future policy with Secretary of State Colin Powell and National Security Adviser Condoleeza Rice. Even so, in the course of the first four months of his secretaryship, still without an adequate staff and fighting to take hold of a massive and famously sluggish bureaucracy, Rumsfeld had more meetings with the joint chiefs of staff than his predecessor, William Cohen, had held in his entire tour of duty.

THE PENTAGON boasts its own internal think tank, called the Office of Net Assessments, which is devoted to examining a whole range of potential threats to the United States and future possibilities for defending against them. The man who heads this office, Andrew Marshall, has been there since the days of the Nixon administration. He is someone who has by now become almost legendary for his ability to be simultaneously hardheaded and visionary (some around the building have nicknamed him "Yoda"). He has also long been known as an advocate of a radical reordering of military organization and policy.

During Rumsfeld's first tour at the Pentagon, Marshall had coauthored a paper with James Roche proposing that the United States establish a long-range, overall strategy for competing with the Soviets and brilliantly detailing the way such a strategy might be brought to bear. It would, said Marshall and Roche, help to rationalize American military planning, which tended to be ad hoc and focused on the near-term. It would also take greater advantage of both American strengths and Soviet weaknesses, which had to that point been sufficiently ignored as to enable the Soviets, with all their economic and manpower difficulties, to achieve rough military parity with the United States. Other problems raised by Marshall and Roche included the country's relations with China and Japan as well as NATO—and more specifically, with France and Germany.

Rumsfeld had been very much impressed with this paper, though he was not in the Pentagon for long enough to do much more than think the issues through. ("The secretary," says Marshall, "has a genuinely strategic kind of mind.") Now, in 2001, Marshall was asked to produce another paper, this one on the role of the U.S. military in the politically, and hence also strategically, transformed post–Cold War world. He handed the paper to the secretary in late March. After this it was distributed among representatives of the armed services, with whom Marshall then held a series of extensive discussions. As he did with a number of selected "outsiders," such as Newt Gingrich and former Defense Secretary James Schlesinger.

Marshall's general idea was that with the Soviet Union gone, the two areas that now posed a potential threat to American tranquility were South Asia (very much including the Middle East—though perhaps even Marshall did not imagine how spectacularly it would soon be coming into play) and the Pacific Rim. It would be impossible to build and maintain large military bases in these regions like those the United States had for more than half a century been maintaining in Germany. Should some problem requiring a military solution arise, it would not be feasible to make use of a massive, World War II–type army: The distances would now be too great to move such a force into the right tactical position with any degree of speed or efficiency. (This had, of course, already happened with the Gulf War of 1991, when six months had been spent amassing an army of 450,000 in the region before military action was taken.)

According to Evan Thomas, commenting on Rumsfeld's relation with the military in the September 11, 2002, issue of *Newsweek,* very soon after the secretary arrived at the Department of Defense he was heard to remark to an aide, "I have just taken Andy Marshall to lunch. I think that'll send a signal." So it did, and Marshall's paper soon set off some alarms within the Pentagon, particularly, for obvious reasons, among the leaders of the army. For of all the branches of service, it was the army to which any alteration of military doctrine based on this kind of analysis would obviously be most disruptive—disruptive both to its habits of thinking and its methods of planning for the future.

Thomas also observed that in the post-Vietnam era many of the army's generals had been acquiring more academic degrees than combat decorations, and that risk had become anathema to a number of rising military stars who were given to worrying that there might be some slipups on their records. As far as Rumsfeld was concerned, this was far from an endearing worry, let alone one deserving more than a possibly minimal drop of sympathy. But it surely played some role in the military's response to the thought of any serious alteration in the distribution of their strategic roles, and thus in the tone of their future relations with the new secretary.

While Marshall was thinking about the larger picture, Rumsfeld also set up a more detailed process of reviewing various military practices and problems, including such things as housing for military families, which had fallen into a scandalous state of shabbiness, and health care, which was fast becoming both an administrative and medical nightmare. Here the review was conducted by means of eighteen separate task forces, which made many people in the building both anxious and suspicious, if not downright bitter. Predictably, some of these people began complaining to Congress, and there were even those who mockingly characterized the review as a military version of Hillary Rodham Clinton's infamous health-care plan.

Some, perhaps hoping against hope or perhaps believing that the wish might be father to the deed, even went so far during that first summer as to spread the rumor that the secretary would imminently be separated from his job.

BECAUSE RUMSFELD'S appointment came late, Bush and Rumsfeld had never had much time for serious private discussions before or during the presidential campaign. But the two men agreed completely about what kind of transformation of the military was required. The armed forces would have to be lighter, faster, more flexible; the various services would need to work together more closely and conduct more joint operations; greater use would have to be made of strategic air power; and in general both doctrine and equipment should be brought more fully into line with the galloping technological advances of the age.

A further problem to be confronted involved what the military call "the teeth-to-tail ratio"—that is, the proportion of people ready for battle to those providing a whole variety of noncombat services. In a significantly reduced force this problem had become all the more severe, with the size of the "tail" entirely disproportionate to the number, and the sharpness, of the "teeth."

Nor were these the only issues that in the secretary's view called for serious attention. Rumsfeld, the maker of lists, is a man who likes to have his problems as well as his possibilities laid out in orderly fashion, and in June he drew up for himself a memo (which he refers to as the "tangled in its own anchor chain" memo) listing a number of things that had gone wrong in the Pentagon over the course of the previous twenty-five years. He noted the fact that there had been an erosion of confidence between the senior military leaders and their subordinates, and that there had been a similar erosion of confidence between members of Congress and the Defense Department. This had resulted in the Pentagon's being burdened by Congress with restrictions and requirements that cut seriously into its ability to manage itself. He then detailed twenty-eight different problems that were impeding the military's ability to be fully effective.

Among these was that by statute the Department of Defense could not reallocate any of the money it might save in one area to use for something else. With a $300 billion budget, for example, it had to get specific congressional approval to put up a needed $500,000 building. Another burden was the requirement that the Department of Defense submit 905 reports to Congress, few of which were read, each and every year. It also had to respond to some 2,500 to 3,000 weekly inquiries or complaints from members of Congress. There was a backlog of about 150,000 security clearances. The department was monitored closely by 24,000 outside auditors and inspectors. It had systems for acquiring personnel that were based on the idea that people enlist for four-year tours rather than for lifetime careers. Its overhead had grown to the point where only an estimated 14 percent of the Department of Defense's manpower was directly related to combat operations. The department maintained processes and regulations so onerous that many commercial businesses working on needed military technologies simply refused to do business with it.

Yet another unfortunate practice was to uproot members of the service (and their families) every few years in order to move them to new assignments, and then to shove many of them out while they are still in their forties. And at a time when the number of those serving in the armed forces has dropped from 2.1 million to 1.4 million, there was a Defense Authorization Bill of some 988 pages—up from 75 pages in 1975 and *1 page* in 1962.

Nor did the foregoing by any means exhaust the secretary's calculation of the problems and outright failures that would have to be addressed if the Defense Department were to be properly reformed.

Though he did not know it then, in only a matter of months the United States would be at war on a far-off and treacherously difficult terrain in a place called Afghanistan—a war that could only be fought properly by a a high-morale, high-performance military force. Rumsfeld was going, as they say, to have his work cut out for him.

M EANWHILE THE Pentagon was abuzz with complaints against Rumsfeld's management style. Years earlier, he had been branded a dangerously skilled bureaucrat by Henry Kissinger—nor had such an idea about him been Kissinger's alone. Later he had been condemned (though also, of course, commended by many of his fellow businessmen) for the brutality of the dispatch with which he had cleaned out the ranks of management at Searle. Even as a congressman, where management was a less relevant issue than in the White House or business, he had been known to his staff as a stickler. From the very beginning, if he were given something written down on paper—an interoffice memo, say, or a letter for his signature—it might be returned to its author many times for correction.

This was the origin of what would come to be known as the "Rumsfeld snowflakes," brief memos requesting revision or amplification of the papers being passed along for his information or approval. Very quickly these "snowflakes" began to fall on various occupants of the Pentagon with blizzard-like abundance, and the irritation and sense of grievance to which they gave rise were made famous all over the city of Washington.

Rumsfeld himself had a very simple explanation of both his manner of dealing with those who were now working for him and his reason for dealing with them in this way: "The Constitution calls for civilian control of this department," he says, "and I'm a civilian." And it had been some time since that control had been exercised. He sometimes, he added, sends back reports as many as seven times before accepting them. "It strikes me that it's terribly important that we do things well and we do things right. I have sent things back on the civilian side as well as the military side. And I will keep right on doing it. We're going to get things done well. It doesn't happen by standing around with your finger in your ear hoping everyone thinks that that's nice."

According to one story that made the rounds of complaint, when Rumsfeld first received a copy of the customary monthly review of U.S. intelligence around the world, which was presented to him in the form of a thick and massively detailed book, he was positively aghast. He said he couldn't believe what he had just been handed. The result was that several Pentagon officials were forced to spend a year turning the review into a slim and readable report. "It was root canal without novocain," one of these officials told a *Los Angeles Times* reporter.

He had, of course, been accruing new wisdoms to be included in his Rules for years. He might now have added to them some formulation of his reason for being so pernickety about what others regarded as no more than routine paperwork: being required to say things precisely also forces people to think about them with some precision.

If the Pentagon provides a far from elegant surrounding for

those who work there, the secretary's office, or rather suite of offices, is, to be sure, suitably grand for the man who presides over the world's most advanced and important military. He works standing up at a tall writing table, as if energy, or perhaps determination, might begin to leak away from too much sitting down. Ernest Hemingway had done his writing in the same way, standing at a tall writing table—though unlike Rumsfeld, he produced at a famously slow pace. Before it slipped away from him, Hemingway had been a man positively obsessed with precision. (In fact, he had to invent a new prose for himself to answer to his ambition to achieve it.) In Rumsfeld's case, though he too is a stickler for clarity and concision, it appears that standing up is the next best thing to forward motion.

As for his insistence on a proper measure of thoughtfulness, there was, for example, the famous and much-debated case of the Crusader, the powerful $23 million battlefield howitzer that was at that point still being designed and that many of the army brass were very keen to have (and that a company called United Defense, located in the state of Oklahoma, was also very keen to produce). There were, in addition, members of Congress, especially Oklahoma Senator James Inhofe, a senior member of the Armed Forces Committee, who were enthusiastic about the weapon.

The trouble was, however, that Crusader would be just too heavy to transport across distances with the speed and efficiency required in wartime. There were other problems with the weapon as well, and the panel tasked with reviewing the program came to the conclusion that it should be canceled. Rumsfeld gave the army three months to come up with an informed and persuasive argument in Crusader's defense, but they were unable to do so; all they could provide was a series of disparate answers to each of the panel's objections.

For a while Crusader became a great *cause célébre* in Washington.

Bets were made, and a number of pundits confidently predicted that Crusader would turn out to be Rumsfeld's Waterloo. They could not, a number of Washington insiders told interviewers, believe that he could succeed in killing the program. For in addition to the Oklahomans, the army—most notably in the persons of Secretary of the Army Thomas White and Chief of Staff General Eric Shinseki—rushed to Capitol Hill, and there the secretary of defense and his associates indeed encountered a pitched battle. "It was," Rumsfeld said of the experience, "as if I had shot a little old lady in the grocery store." In the end, Crusader and its supporters lost, and the program was dropped. Later Rumsfeld would observe that the battle over Crusader had been "more important not to lose than it was to win[3]."

Something similar happened with Vieques, the island six miles off the coast of Puerto Rico that the navy had been using for bombing practice since the 1940s (and had also later rented to NATO for the same purpose). The natives of Vieques had for some years been strenuously demanding that the bombing stop and the navy decamp. For one thing, they argued, their health was being seriously impaired and this was clearly an effect of environmental problems caused by the bombings. Moreover, the island's economy, which, they claimed, might otherwise have been booming with tourism, was virtually nonexistent. At first, the navy had resisted this pressure—mainly because Vieques was in many respects an ideal place to train—but on April 7, 2003, they would indeed clear off the island, never to return. One of the reasons for Rumsfeld's decision

---

[3] Though after some time White would "resign" and Shinseki's tour as chief of staff would come to an end, immediately after this battle both men remained in their jobs. Some of their more bitter opponents feared that this was too great a kindness on the secretary's part. But they were very likely mistaken: to have been required to remain at the site of so marked a defeat might well have felt to these men like not much of a kindness at all.

was that when he requested the navy to present the argument for continuing to use the island, it had proved unable to muster a sufficiently persuasive case.

None of this, it goes without saying, was calculated to endear the secretary to certain important members, whether lay or military, of the Pentagon population. At one point, the joint chiefs of staff were even said to have held a closed meeting devoted entirely to a scathing discussion of his methods and intentions. And some members and hangers-on of this population—particularly among the retired brass and certain civilian employees of the Department of Defense with civil-service tenure—would in fact never stop airing their grievances.

On the other hand, it did not take all that long for the people who spent the most time with Rumsfeld to come to understand his management style, which was characterized as equal parts debating club and wrestling match. "He takes a strong position for people to shoot at," one of them told the *New York Times*. "But if you challenge it, you must be prepared to be cross-examined in a manner that someone has referred to as 'the wire brush treatment.'" Others spoke of the process as "death by a thousand questions. He keeps people off-guard. But that's how he gets better work from them."

His own account of how he and his associates ultimately reach agreement is by means of "a process where everyone is learning and everyone is contributing. By the time you end up with a product, it's almost impossible to know who it came from or how it evolved." Such a process naturally requires people who are both strong of mind and fully at ease in the precincts of ego. As it happens, digging up and surrounding himself with people like this is one of Rumsfeld's special talents.

R UMSFELD WAS not in the least surprised by the discord he encountered during those early months in the Pentagon. How could he have been? After all, his years as a businessman had left him well-acquainted with the cost in the coin of popularity that resulted from imposing one's authority over a large and complicated enterprise. Now, in undertaking nothing less than a refashioning of the armed forces of the United States—their thinking, their equipment, and the way they would organize themselves for going into battle if battle there was to be—he was imposing his authority over a much larger and far more complicated enterprise.

There would come the day, some two years down the road, when those whose resistance he had successfully put down would set out to exact their revenge by attacking his plan for the conduct of the approaching war in Iraq. In the meantime, Rumsfeld pushed ahead.

During one of their early conversations he told the president, "If you want me to change the building, I'll change the building." But possibly the most important aspect of the change he would bring about in the Pentagon was not located in the particulars of his reform. Rather it consisted in the reassertion of the principle—as he would say over and over—set down in the Constitution that the military was to remain under the control of the citizens of the United States in the person of their president.

If Rumsfeld had not been so naive as to be shocked or upset by the inevitable resistance to his mission in the Pentagon this second time around, he was unprepared for the refusal of Congress to grant him the kind of support he needed. This might seem strange for someone who had himself once been a member of that body—though in a different time, and with the country in a different condition. In any event, possibly for no better reason than that he still had friends there, Rumsfeld had expected that his determination to effect reform of the military would find backing on Capitol Hill.

Instead, Congress proved almost as great an obstacle to what he trying to accomplish as his opponents in the Pentagon.

In any case, during the course of the summer of 2001—call it the summer of his discontent—he confided to a friend that his only recourse might be to go over the heads of Congress and try to reach the American people.

He could not have imagined how soon he would be afforded the opportunity to do just that.

Back to basics, aboard Max

A CHANGE IN

THE WEATHER

T HEN CAME September 11.

Overnight the whole country was awakened to the very danger that Rumsfeld had spoken of for so long and to so little effect: the danger of a terrorist attack on American soil. And with that awakening the country was also caught up in a wave of emotion that took most people, if not indeed everyone, by surprise. As the twin towers of New York's World Trade Center crumbled and the ashes left behind in the conflagration began to settle, the United States was awash from sea to shining sea not only in feelings of rediscovered brotherhood and

At the White House (left to right): *General Myers, Bush, Cheney, Andrew Card, Rumsfeld, Condoleeza Rice, Paul Wolfowitz*

shared grief but of a newfound patriotic fervor such as had not been seen in more than half a century.

Thus for well over a year after September 11, American flags were flying from virtually every post and parapet, car, bus, and boat dock in the land, and it seemed that no public meeting or banquet could begin or conclude without a heartfelt rendition of the Irving Berlin anthem, *God Bless America.*

These groundswells of patriotism signaled the end of a time of taking the country's bounteous good fortune for granted. The world had all too suddenly become a dangerous place for ordinary Americans, and people's hearts turned homeward with a new-found fervor.

Along with this swell of sentiment there came a firm popular embrace of George W. Bush. The president responded to the out-rage of that September morning with a satisfyingly commensurate sense of outrage, and what was perhaps even more important, he promised that the country would speedily be avenged. Both of these emotions, outrage and the determination to be avenged, were what large numbers of people needed to hear expressed, and they began showering the president with their approval (a shower that would continue through and beyond the elections of 2002, when on his account they gave his party a virtually unprecedented midterm victory).

Rumsfeld had, of course, given a great deal of thought to the problem of terrorism and how to fight it. "It is not possible," he has said, "to defend against terrorism in every place, at every time, against every conceivable technique. Self-defense against terrorism requires preemption, taking the battle to the terrorists wherever they are and to those who harbor them." Moreover, "The link be-tween global terrorist networks and the nations on the terrorist list that have active weapons-of-mass-destruction capabilities is real, and poses a serious threat to the world."

I T WAS not only Bush, however, but Donald Rumsfeld, too—or perhaps in a way Donald Rumsfeld most especially—for whom September 11 marked the beginning of yet another unforeseeable change. For while he had not yet really begun to deliver on his ambition to bring the United States armed forces out of the Cold War and into the strategically transformed and high-tech world of the twenty-first century, some—in the end, a good deal—of the resistance to him was soon to give way.

There was something else, too, that resulted in a lowering of resistance. On that fateful morning of September 11, only minutes after American Airlines flight number 77 crashed into the east wall of the Pentagon, Rumsfeld was seen hurrying outside and rushing toward the section of the building that was now on fire. There he grabbed hold of a stretcher and began to help with the job of carrying the wounded out of and away from the building. He continued to haul stretchers until someone came outside to pull him back indoors and into a safe room. Neither Rumsfeld's close friends nor, certainly, his wife would have been in the least surprised by this behavior. But now the word began to spread throughout the Pentagon, particularly among some of the younger officers: The secretary may make you sweat, they were saying, but he is also ready to lay himself and his body on the line for you.

Soon thereafter Rumsfeld instituted the practice of holding town meetings every few months with the people who were working in the building. After each one of these meetings, at which he would speak and then answer questions, it would take Rumsfeld at least half an hour to get back to his office, so intent were those present to shake his hand or, better yet, to have their pictures taken with him.

To add to this change of atmosphere, on October 1 the president replaced the then-current chairman of the joint chiefs of staff, Henry Shelton, with Air Force General Richard B. Myers. Myers, who had been vice chairman, was in turn replaced in that position by General Peter Pace (the first marine general ever to serve in this job). From the beginning, Rumsfeld, Myers, and Pace worked together in a refreshing spirit of collegiality—and even fun. "Myers created a presence that was solid and rooted," Rumsfeld said of him. "We had to do a lot of things on the fly, and the two of us just sat down and worked out the rules of engagement. He's intelligent, he's quick, and he also has a very good sense of humor."

If all was not yet perfectly peaceful in the secretary's surroundings[1], a great stride had now been made in that direction. There were, to be sure, certain remaining pockets of resistance in the imaginary but well-worn pathway that stretches between the Pentagon and the Capitol. At least for now, however, the main warfare was reserved for the terrorists of Al Qaeda and their hosts, the Taliban government of Afghanistan.

Myers, whom the public would come to know well through his participation in many if not most of Rumsfeld's press briefings in the Pentagon, was regarded within the military as a bit of a maverick: He was an air force man who (like the secretary) was a proponent of weapons in space. He was also an advocate of testing and building defenses against weapons called "laser dazzlers," being developed by the Chinese among others, and of the use of cyberwarfare. And, not irrelevant as far as some observers were concerned, he was also known to possess considerable political skill. The question was, on whose side would he be throwing his considerable weight? It was a question that would take no time to answer. But in

---

[1] While those with complaints against Rumsfeld were never shy about making their feelings known, he himself steadfastly refused not only to repay them in kind but even to acknowledge that such things caused him any difficulties.

any case, within a week of his ascension to the chairmanship, there would be a war on.

ASIDE FROM its effect on the atmosphere in the country in general and in the Pentagon in particular, September 11 also marked the start of Donald Rumsfeld's unexpected life as a national celebrity. Indeed, even more than a national celebrity—and even more unexpected—he soon became a media hero for numbers of American men and a kind of pinup for countless American (and not only American) women—almost without regard to political leanings. People would stop him in public places, interrupt him at dinner in restaurants, and in general treat him rather more like a Hollywood star than like an important government official.

It all came about as a result of the televised briefings he frequently gave to the Pentagon press corps, especially when the country went to war in Afghanistan. At that point Rumsfeld's briefings made him the chief public exponent and explainer of the war. And he conducted them with a candor so uncommon to the usual public demeanor of a public official, and at the same time with so much wit and panache, that what came to be known as the "Rummy Show" was soon playing to ever larger and ever more appreciative audiences.

It is often hard to tell just what it is that draws the attention and admiration of the public (if movie producers knew what it was, they would all be among the world's most secure billionaires instead of among its most foolhardy gamblers). But it must be the case, at least sometimes, that what else is afoot in people's lives—such as a war, or a depression, or a run of economic good fortune—has much to do with what they find enlightening and/or entertaining. September 11 certainly touched a deep national nerve. Still, that the mantle of media hero should have been placed on the shoulders of the country's secretary of defense was after all an extraordinary development.

Rumsfeld's predecessor, William Cohen, for instance, had in the course of his four years in the Pentagon held some three dozen press conferences that were carried on cable television, but to very little, if any, general notice. During that time the United States had even been engaged in military action, in response to the Serbian onslaught against the Kosovars. Furthermore, U.S. policy in Kosovo had stirred a great deal of public argument and heated controversy in the press. Even so, however, the public had not really been stirred: Vast numbers of Americans, including writers for the country's elite publications, seemed far more eager to keep in

touch with President Clinton's private peccadilloes than with their country's engagements and intentions abroad.

The office that Cohen then occupied was established in September 1947, and there have to date been twenty men serving in it (Rumsfeld is designated the twenty-first secretary because this is his second appointment to the job). Some of these men have been powerful, some merely well-connected. Some of them have been regarded as shrewd, some even as brilliant. But whatever may have been the romantic standing of any such individual figure among the women of his private acquaintance, it would have been difficult, if not impossible, to imagine that he would have been selected by a popular magazine as one of the year's leading sex heroes. Yet this was precisely the title conferred upon Rumsfeld by the editors of *People* in an issue of November 2002. Among other explanations offered for this choice, the magazine quoted Henry Kissinger's famous remark, "Power is the ultimate aphrodisiac." Which, like its author, is clever and may also have the virtue of being true. But for the most part, with the exception of people who are either professionally engaged in or privately passionate about politics, perceptions of power where the government is concerned tend to focus on the president rather than on the members of his cabinet (except, of course, for Kissinger himself). Nor has the Pentagon ever carried anything like a romantic aura.

But here was Rumsfeld, quite suddenly being designated by the media "a virtual rock star" (CNN), a "babe magnet" (Fox), and "the new hunk of homefront airtime" (the *Wall Street Journal*). Even the president would join the chorus, teasingly addressing his secretary of defense as "Rumstud." What made this all the more re-

Meeting with the sultan of Oman in his summer tent city, just before the war in Afghanistan

markable was that the new heartthrob, placed in *People*'s pantheon of erotic heroism among the likes of Ben Affleck, Mel Gibson, Hugh Grant, George Clooney, and Julio Iglesias, was a man now seventy years old, married for some forty-eight years to his high-school sweetheart, the father of two grown daughters and a son and the grandfather of five (soon then to be six) grandchildren. ("Do you *realize*," his fifteen-year-old granddaughter demanded of her mother, "that his picture is on the page of this magazine opposite Tom Cruise? *Tom Cruise,* mother.")

Aside from *People* and the good-humored effusions of the likes of Fox and the *Wall Street Journal,* he would in the not too distant future achieve what some would regard as the ultimate in celebrity status by being portrayed in a skit on *Saturday Night Live.* According to Darrell Hammond, the man chosen to mimic him, Rumsfeld's manner was reminiscent of that of Henry Fonda playing Tom Joad in the movie *The Grapes of Wrath.* That was a curious response to someone so confident of what he is about as Rumsfeld. Even more curious was Hammond's observation that at times, as he told the *New York Observer,* Rumsfeld can appear more "tightly wound than Aaron Brown after one thousand Red Bulls." People who don't watch press conferences, Hammond said, watch Rumsfeld's, and so does he. (He played Rumsfeld that way, but it is not likely that either Hammond himself or the rest of Rumsfeld's audience would actually continue to watch much give-and-take on what are after all matters of life and death between members of the press and someone as "tightly wound" as Hammond described. Actually, he is relaxed, though sometimes stern for effect, and seldom, though perhaps on occasion, genuinely irritated.)

Be that as it may, there was no question that Rumsfeld, as he had only recently imagined he might have to do, would now be going over the heads of Congress and reaching the American people.

T HE PROCESS began roughly on Sunday, October 7, 2001, when Rumsfeld and General Myers mounted the podium in the briefing room of the Pentagon to announce that the United States had that day gone to war in Afghanistan. The aim of the war the two men had come to announce was, of course, to destroy the heart and nerve center of the Al Qaeda terrorist conspiracy—in other words, the authors of September 11—along with the Taliban government of Afghanistan that had for so long granted the terrorists the freedom of their country. The hostilities, said Rumsfeld, had commenced with a series of bombings intended as a first move to knock out the Taliban air force, which would then give America's allies among the Afghanis the freedom to move around the country. President Bush had made the decision to use military force, he continued, in order to complement the already ongoing worldwide economic, financial, and diplomatic efforts to raise the terrorists' costs of doing business.

Rumsfeld declared that the United States stood with the people of Afghanistan who were being oppressed by their government, a government that also gave houseroom to those who engaged in acts of terror and murder all over the world. In stressing that we were at war with the Taliban regime and not the people of Afghanistan, Rumsfeld was sounding a refrain that he would repeat over and over again in relation to yet another country, Iraq, with which the United States would in the not too distant future also be at war. It was important, he would later say, to emphasize to the Afghanis that the United States was not there to stay, but rather to help fight terrorism and liberate the Afghan people from Al Qaeda and the Taliban and make sure that that a new Afghan government had the opportunity to succeed.

Seated before the secretary and the chairman that day were the journalists assigned to cover defense and military issues for a variety of media, including newspapers, syndicates, radio, and TV networks. When the time came for questions, the reporters immediately adopted the challenging posture and tone that had long been standard practice in press briefings with government officials: Can you describe the covert operation? Do you plan to have many troops on the ground? Did you target Al Qaeda leader Usama Bin Laden? And so on. Rumsfeld had also mentioned in the course of his opening statement that the United States intended to distribute food and medicine to the suffering Afghani people, and someone asked, "How big has this humanitarian effort been thus far? How many tons are you trying to deliver?"

These were odd questions to ask on the first day of a war— some of them, indeed, on any day of a war. Probably the journalists attending the briefing could as yet think of no others: It was too early for there to be real news, and yet they were after all trying to earn their keep as reporters. Be that as it may, on that day the journalists' questions generally produced one- or two-syllable answers from Rumsfeld: "Yes," "No," "Too soon." The question about the covert operation did occasion a rather weary reminder by the secretary that the word *covert* precisely meant the opposite of *overt* and thus he would simply not answer.

The final query of that day was, as the earlier ones had in fact not been, forthrightly hostile and asked in a hostile tone: "We hear that the electricity is out in Kabul. Are you not running the risk of being thought the enemies of the Afghan people?" To which Rumsfeld, sighing deeply, replied: "You know, in this world of ours if you get up in the morning, you run the risk of having someone lie about you or mischaracterize what it is you are doing." A few minutes later, he and Myers left the press room.

Rumsfeld would from then on be giving a great many such briefings. And if on October 7, 1991, the reporters had not yet fully taken his measure, it appears that by the end of that day's session he had quite brilliantly taken theirs. No matter how consuming of his time and concern it was to keep track of a faraway war, and though he would on grounds of national security sometimes simply refuse to answer, he would henceforth rarely respond to their questions with real—though now and then, to be sure, with feigned—impatience. Nor for the most part would he permit himself to betray any sign of genuine irritation with a reporter (though, again, he would from time to time make very good use of certain gestures of irritation for effect).

All this, however, was not the result of his having set out on the one hand to manipulate, or on the other hand to please, the press, but precisely because he hadn't. Now, whereas in some other countries rudeness is the weapon of first recourse, Americans do not like to be in the presence of rudeness; it makes them uncomfortable. As many foreigners have attested, Americans are on the whole the most polite people in the world, particularly to strangers. But neither do they like even the suggestion of cowardice or toadying. Rumsfeld managed to strike just the right balance—to judge from the enthusiasm of the response to him a balance not often encountered—among tough, straightforward, kindly, amused, and deadly sincere.

Before very long these press briefings were taking on something of the character of a sports event. Which is to say, they began to assume the rhythm of an ongoing game: a pitching, or perhaps hitting, duel between the most valuable player in the major leagues and a group of kids from the knothole gang who both love to watch him play and wish they could now and then earn a little glory by tripping him up. To be sure, a couple of the reporters remained steadfastly more interested in the tripping up than in the admiring aspect of this game, but by and large it rather quickly became a sporting affair. Which was why it made for such good television.

The things about which Rumsfeld was mainly required to provide information were deadly serious: danger, warfare, bombing, killing. But while sometimes the atmosphere in the briefing room would become very solemn, the mood never seemed to descend to grimness—as it has with relative frequency, for instance, during White House briefings on other less than happy subjects. Rumsfeld would say only what he was ready or able to say, the reporters would try to push him to give them more, he would sometimes then respond by teasing them (in which case there would be a good deal of laughter) or by being moved to eloquence (in which case there would follow a moment or two of quiet).

Rumsfeldian eloquence is itself a most interesting phenomenon. It neither comes off as self-consciously scripted—like that of Adlai Stevenson, for instance, from whom Rumsfeld claims to have received much inspiration—nor is it spun out of a deep literary tradition like that of the late Daniel P. Moynihan. Nor, certainly, does it bear much relation to the high wit and troubled spirit that were combined in that most eloquent of all American leaders (who was also one of the greatest masters of American prose), Abraham Lincoln.

At a town meeting with the people at Nellis Air Force base in February 2002, Rumsfeld was asked how the government meant to protect its military bases from terrorist attack. His answer: "You and I know that the only way you can deal with terrorists is to go after them. The only defense against terrorism is offense. It is preemption. It is finding them and rooting them out and stopping them. And it's dealing with the countries that harbor them."

Not a government-issue or politician-style euphemism in a

carload. Indeed, Rumsfeld might at first seem to be merely plain-spoken. Though he is, to be sure, "merely" nothing of the kind. When he wants to, he can say what is on his mind with a deceptive, almost boyish, simplicity—sometimes punctuated with such old-style midwesternisms as "Oh, my goodness," "Gosh," and "You bet"—that there can never be any doubt of his intention. The press can misquote him, but reporters, or anyone else for that matter, cannot with any degree of innocence mistake his meaning. By the same token, he can when he wants to slip effortlessly right out of a questioner's grasp. And this was something immediately under-stood, and just as immediately applauded, by the general public. In the words of Fox TV's Tony Snow, "He doesn't act like somebody who's been trained to come on TV. A guy who probably would shock and horrify every media trainer is a reporter's dream."

RUMSFELD IS a man given not only to collecting "rules" and "brilliant pebbles" but also, as has been mentioned, to draw-ing up lists—lists of problems, lists of accomplishments, and lists of principles. In March of 2002 he set down a list of "Principles for the Department of Defense," clearly drawn up in response to the experience of being at war. Among other things, some of them shed a particularly interesting light on his methods with the press. "Do nothing," the list of principles begins, "that could raise ques-tions about the credibility of DoD. DoD officials must tell the truth and must be believed to be telling the truth or our important work is undermined." Another of these principles begins, "Do nothing that is or could be seen as partisan. The work of this Department is nonpartisan." Still another is, "The public needs and has a right to know about the unprivileged and unclassified ac-tivities of DoD. It is our obligation to provide that information professionally, fully, and in good spirit." "Reflect the compassion we all feel when lives are lost, whether U.S. or coalition service people or innocents killed by collateral damage." "Demonstrate our appreciation for the cooperation we receive from other nations and for the valuable contributions coalition forces bring to our efforts. . . ." "The legislative branch is in Article I of the Constitution; the executive branch is Article II. That is not an accident." And "Finally, the president of the United States is our commander-in-chief. Those of us in DoD—military and civilian—believe in civilian control, are respectful of it, and must be vigilant

to see that our actions reflect that important Constitutional obligation." The rest of the principles pertain to what might be called intra-Pentagon relations and attitudes, and together they make up a rather precise rendering of Rumsfeld's own methods as a briefer of the press.

The Pentagon journalists who dealt with him regularly seemed rather quickly to take the measure of those methods and for the most part got into the spirit of the exchange with him. But interviewers in the general press and on television talk shows who were being no more than the slightest bit professionally hostile to him, especially after he would slam down the lid on some question of theirs, would often have to fish around quickly to find a new topic of discussion.

There was a good example of this on a Sunday morning interview with Tim Russert of *Meet the Press* during the run-up to the war in Iraq. The Pope, in a plea that the United States refrain from going to war in Iraq, had said, "Whoever decides that all peaceful means available under international law are exhausted assumes a grave responsibility before God, his own conscience, and history." Russert, in an unmistakable spirit of challenge, read this statement to Rumsfeld and asked him what he thought of it, and to his visible astonishment Rumsfeld answered with perfect aplomb, "The Pope is right."

"What? You *agree* with him?" Russert's voice seemed to rise a full octave.

"It's true," came back the unhesitating answer. "War is the last choice."

Press conference in Kabul with Hamid Karzai (center) *and Defense Minister Mohammed Qasin Fahim Khan*

It is hard to think of anyone else in Rumsfeld's position who might have turned that particular table with that particular kind of ease.

Be his technique for doing so as it may, whichever way the conversation goes, he almost always ends up in control of it. Anyone who might imagine that this is a simple or unartful way of communicating with the world had better learn to keep his hand on his wallet.

T HE QUESTION remains, how did the wider public suddenly "discover" this new figure, a man who had off and on been in public view for forty years? Because the country was at war, it was natural that the secretary of defense should be interviewed fairly often in the newspapers and on the networks. In that sense, he was rather fully on display. But for many of those who were to become his devoted fans, it was the Pentagon press briefings that had led to the discovery of his art. Still, the briefings were for the most part being broadcast in full only on C-Span, a cable channel that boasts what is probably the most loyal audience in the country but one that by TV standards could hardly be called massive. (Well more than a year later, when the United States was still mopping up in Afghanistan and at the same time seeking to destroy the regime of Saddam Hussein, the briefings would often be aired on Fox News, as well.)

In short, Rumsfeld's newfound stardom must have had a great deal to do with the phenomenon that the publicists call "word of mouth." And for those in the Pentagon who were still seething

With Pakistani president Pervez Musharraf

over Rumsfeld's reassessment of military doctrine and practice—
and for their friends and allies among the retired military—the
stardom of this secretary can only have poured additional salt on
open wounds.

THERE HAD not been much time to think about or plan for
going to war in Afghanistan. After all, the sheer dimension of
what took place on September 11 called for the United States to
make both a quick and an unmistakable response. Thus the discus-

sions between the president and the national security team about
when and how to go after Al Qaeda and the Taliban were very intense. As described in his usual "I-am-the-man/I-was-there" detail
by Bob Woodward in *Bush At War,* these consultations ended with
a reasonably cheerful consensus. There would first of all be a coalition made up of countries willing to contribute to the anti-terrorist
effort in various ways. Moreover, the CIA, which had for a long
time been maintaining "assets" in Afghanistan, would essentially
buy the military services of certain tribal leaders ready to stage an
insurrection against the Taliban, while the United States and Great
Britain, with guidance from U.S. Special Forces on the ground,

would conduct a high-tech air war. But there were, in the old infantry parlance, to be relatively few American or coalition "boots on the ground."

Rumsfeld later said he recognized that the U.S. military was finally adapting to a new and different kind of world in the twenty-first century when one day he received a requisition for saddles and stirrups. What this meant, he explained, was that the military had come to understand how a single soldier mounted on an old mule could, by riding up one of Afghanistan's hills on the animal and using a Global Positioning (GPS) device, call down air strikes on the enemy with perfect accuracy.

Afghanistan being a country whose difficult terrain has down through history been its greatest protection, the original plan for conducting the war wound up, as such plans almost always do, going through a fair amount of revision and adaptation to unforeseen developments. The Russians had tried to move in on that country as recently as December 1979, and despite their preponderance of military power, had come a cropper in trying to deal with Afghanistan's grueling geography and the people who were at home in its crags and crannies. Clearly, something quite different from and beyond a conventional invasion and head-on military action was needed, and it was in fact provided.

Even so, both the plan discussed in the White House and the subsequent revisions of it had their critics, perhaps most hostile among them R. W. Apple of the *New York Times*. But since the capital, Kabul, was taken after only six weeks (and the important city of Mazar-I-Sharif brought under control one week later), and with preparations for the creation of a new representative government of Afghanistan already in process, the critics were unable to make

After-dinner conversation in Kuwait

much of an issue of their reservations. Certainly, to judge by the polls, they made no great headway with the general public.

This criticism of the war had basically taken two forms. First, it was asked, in view of the fact that Afghanistan had defeated the might of the Russian army, what gave us the right to believe that we could succeed where the Russians had failed. (This was the "quagmire" objection, borrowed by R. W. Apple with only a little adaptation from the days of Vietnam.) But then, as the military effort began to show signs of succeeding, the complaint became that coalition forces were failing in the main purpose of going into Afghanistan in the first place, which was to catch Usama Bin Laden and the other top leaders of Al Qaeda.

Meanwhile, however, in liberated Kabul people literally dug up out of their backyards the buried television sets and VCRs that the Taliban had forbidden them to watch and, to the accompaniment of the music that the Taliban had forbidden them to hear, they began to dance in the streets. Moreover, as soon as word spread that the Taliban were out and the Americans were in, each day thousands of Afghan refugees who had been living in camps in Pakistan began pouring back home, women were freely walking in the streets again, and young Afghanis would soon be in school. It did not take long for the voices of the critics to be drowned out by the sounds and sights of success.

The war in Afghanistan nevertheless went on in some fashion long after the United States became embroiled in another war. For the Taliban and especially Al Qaeda continued to make trouble, slipping back and forth across Afghanistan's unmanageably porous borders and finding succor and support among certain of Afghanistan's neighbors.

Hence questions about Usama Bin Laden, where he was thought to be and when they might expect him to be killed or taken, remained a constant weekly hum of implicit complaint. (At

one point, Rumsfeld even humorously complained that his wife had begun to badger him with it.) Yet only a very few members of the Pentagon press corps ever signaled that they thought Rumsfeld might not be telling them the whole truth: How could they, when he dealt with them by simply refusing to answer the questions that he either could not, should not, or did not wish to, answer—and dealing fully with the questions that he could and did wish to answer?

Nevertheless, the game would soon be moving into a new, and a rather different, inning.

8

PUSH COMES TO SHOVE

O N MARCH 20, 2003, Rumsfeld and Richard Myers once again strode into the Pentagon's press room to announce that the United States was at war, this time against Iraq. Or, to be more precise, the United States was at war against the Saddam Hussein regime in Iraq. For, as Rumsfeld emphasized, it was not the people of that country but only their leader and his murderous Baathist underlings whom the United States and its allies were undertaking to destroy.

Some Americans had been expressing the fear that such a war would not defeat the country's enemies but only create more of them—especially on that potentially explosive mythical terrain called the "Arab street." Others, many fewer but as usual far nois-

Town meeting in Doha, Qatar, with ENTCOM commander General Tommy Franks, December 2002

ier, were once again suggesting that *no* war fought by the United States could be legitimate. But the polls revealed that most Americans accepted the view of the president, his secretary of defense, his national security adviser, and even to some extent by now his secretary of state that going into Iraq was a necessary continuation of the war on terrorism: in this case against a regime that was dangerous less because it harbored movements trained and armed for suicide bombings than because it maintained an arsenal of weapons of mass destruction that it could, and very likely would, make available to such movements.

This was the second time in a year and a half that Rumsfeld and Myers had come to this place and stood before these journalists and cameras to announce that the country was now at war. And like their earlier announcement, made hard on the heels of 9/11, this one, too, could have come as no surprise to anyone. Over the course of the previous six months President George W. Bush and his diplomatic minions had been unsuccessfully pressing the United Nations Security Council either to take, or at least to approve, some action against Iraq. For nearly twelve years, the United Nations had been pressing Saddam Hussein to give up his country's weapons of mass destruction. The security council had passed a number of resolutions demanding that the weapons be destroyed and had bootlessly sent teams of inspectors to Iraq to make sure that they were destroyed. Sanctions had been imposed. Diplomatic missions had trooped to Baghdad to urge Saddam to comply. All to no effect: Though he had already used poison gas, both in his war against Iran and against the Kurds in his own country, Saddam Hussein continued to deny that he had any such weapons, first playing a game of "find them if you can" with the inspectors, then throwing them out of the country, and then allowing them back in to go around the same track again.

Finally, in September 2002, George W. Bush had entered the fray, taking himself off to New York in order to give the UN one last chance to make good on its own declared policy. Beyond this effort, and as an earnest of America's intention to seek out and eliminate those weapons along with the regime that had so long defied its own agreement not to produce them, American forces had been deployed in the region and American ships had been sent to stand by in both the Persian Gulf and the Mediterranean. For half a year or more Bush had continued warning Saddam Hussein that his only alternatives to war were to give a truthful accounting of the weapons or leave Iraq and go into exile. By the last week of March, since diplomacy had not availed either at the United Nations or with Saddam Hussein himself, and since the intolerably brutal Iraqi summer would soon be upon the forces gathering nearby, both time and Bush's patience had run out.

Except for the few Americans who can always be counted on to say no to any and every use of military power by their own country, there had been little of anything resembling a public debate about going into Afghanistan. Less than a month had gone by after 9/11, and the country was still in a high fever of shock, rage, loss, and love when that war started. This time, however, conditions were very different. At home, the flags, though still in evidence, were no longer flying so ubiquitously, the decals shouting "Let's roll!" were fading on the car bumpers, the passion aroused by the World Trade Center was now for the most part only local and was mainly centered on the issue of what to do about replacing it. Politicians were once again wooing voters with the usual promises, and people had to a considerable extent returned to their own private concerns. Abroad, many of the countries that had in the autumn of 2001 expressed sympathy for America's pain and had pledged to take part in the war against terrorism now refused to endorse any move against Iraq. It seems that Afghanistan may have been one thing, but an oil-rich Arab country smack in the heart of the Middle East was something else again.

It seems safe to say that few Americans beside the members of the country's diplomatic corps found the security council's immobility more than an accustomed irritant—most ordinary citizens having long ceased paying much attention, if indeed any, to the UN. It was simply there, on the shore of the East River in New York City, and going its own way almost entirely out of public view and quite out of mind. But there was a good deal of simple outrage

at the discovery that among those most noisily refusing to support the United States on this issue were France and Germany—countries, it was said over and over, who owed their own present freedom and good fortune to the fact that Americans had once fought and died on their soil. (This resentment would soon boil over into an unorganized and entirely informal boycott of things French that would, in only a few months, cost the French wine industry untold millions of dollars in exports to the United States.)

But even as hostility to France and Germany was spreading, the opposition to Bush and his views being expressed with so much disdain by the leaders of these countries was being used by those in the United States itself who were also opposed to an invasion of Iraq. Demonstrations against military action began to crop up on university campuses and in various American cities, and the usual complement of show business and literary celebrities waxed passionate about keeping the peace in their usual flamboyant, mock-outraged manner.

Rumsfeld himself rather notoriously stepped into the controversy about America's former allies now turned opponents. At a press briefing in late January, a Dutch journalist asked him what he made of the fact that so many Europeans would now rather give the benefit of the doubt to Saddam Hussein than to President George Bush. To which, after a brief and rather deft little speech on the difficulty of achieving unanimity in this world, Rumsfeld replied: "Now, you're thinking of Europe as Germany and France. I don't. I think that's old Europe. If you look at the entire NATO Europe today, you will see that the center of gravity is shifting to the east. . . . If you just take the list of all the members of NATO

"What is your question?"

and all of those who have been invited in recently—What is it, twenty-six, something like that?—you're right. Germany has been a problem, and France has been a problem."

The responding anger on the part of both the Europeans and their sympathizers in the United States was so great that one might have thought he had said that Germany had become nothing more than a land of beer swillers and France a country of cowards. Not only in France and Germany but throughout Europe the press devoted pages and pages to expressing outrage. Even the prime minister of America's ally Spain, Jose Maria Aznar, cautioned Bush while on a visit to the president's ranch in Crawford, Texas, that he had better put a muzzle on his defense secretary. "I did tell the president," said Aznar, "that we need a lot of Powell and not much of Rumsfeld." (When asked about Aznar's remark later, Rumsfeld laughed and said, "Oh, heck, he's a fine man and he's been a good supporter, and everyone is entitled to his own opinion. The president of the United States has certainly never said anything like that to me.") To add to the brouhaha, a group of the secretary's relatives in Germany, who had only recently been boasting of their connection with him, now declared that they no longer considered him a member of their family.

Like most press "events" in the United States this one had its days of white heat and then disappeared behind some blast of new and equally momentary heat to come. The effect that lingered was mainly a large and amused seconding of the secretary's position on the matter. No poll seems to have been taken at that moment, but had it been, "old Europe" would undoubtedly have produced a dramatic increase in what was already an unusually high Rumsfeld approval rating.

"Other politicians sweat for weeks over a major ninety-minute speech, hire the best writers, craft memorable phrases, and nobody notices," a columnist calling himself "The Straight Talker" wrote in the London *Daily Telegraph*. "If you want to 'reshape the debate,' as the cliché has it, all you need is a casual aside from Rummy. The concept of 'old Europe' barely existed until Rumsfeld used it as a throwaway line a month and a half ago. Within a week, it became the dominant regional paradigm."

Indeed, far from subsiding, on the continent anger about "old Europe" was from the look of things going to continue for years and years. What was especially interesting about this brouhaha were two things most vividly revealed by it. The first was the depth of French and German rage at the discrepancy between America's power and their own. (They had not reacted this way to Afghanistan, but then the war in Afghanistan had arisen precisely from an incident of American powerlessness.) And second was the glimpse it afforded of a growing hostility to Donald Rumsfeld, not only among his old opponents in the military and now in Western Europe, but also among certain members of the American press, reporters and especially columnists, who seemed to have been waiting for a chance to record that the secretary had at last fallen on his face.

So eager were they to discredit Rumsfeld that they even set aside their normally unfriendly attitude toward the army and turned themselves into conduits for the arguments against him coming from retired generals still carrying their old grievances (and ready to express dissatisfaction with the war plan for Iraq). But some of the press's growing hostility also involved Rumsfeld's starring role in an administration that had in the view of many reporters stolen the election from their preferred candidate. And some may even have been the result of boredom: like the Lord, the press giveth and the press taketh away.

The State Department, too, joined in the fray. Powell "let it be known," as they say in diplomatic circles, that he was furious at

Rumsfeld's remark for having stiffened French and German opposition to the resolution authorizing a war on Iraq that he was then seeking from the UN Security Council. And the *New York Times* quoted an "anonymous friend" of Powell's as saying, "Diplomacy is slipping away and Rumsfeld needs some duct tape put over his mouth."

Still, while some of his American critics continued referring to it, the carry-on over "Old Europe" did not really prove to be the opportunity sought by anyone out to do him and his reputation serious harm. On this side of the Atlantic, where Rumsfeld after all had serious work to be getting on with, his remark had both passed too quickly and had been much too enthusiastically embraced by the American public. Juicier opportunities, however, would soon be provided by the war in Iraq.

B Y THE time Rumsfeld and Myers arrived at the press room on March 20, the announcement they had come to make was no longer news. The president had issued Saddam an ultimatum giving him forty-eight hours either to comply with the UN resolutions or get out of the country, and he had not responded. Making good on Bush's ultimatum, Tomahawk missiles had been launched the previous night (afternoon in the Eastern United States and noon in California) from six United States warships against a certain building compound in the city of Baghdad. This compound was one known to be used by senior members of the

Allies: taking questions from the press with Prime Minister John Howard of Australia

regime, and Central Command in Doha, Qatar, had received a last-minute piece of intelligence that Saddam Hussein himself would be there at the time. Simultaneously, Iraqi air-defense systems, surface-to-surface missiles, and artillery batteries were attacked from the air.

Although it was hard to make out any of the details from the very limited camera coverage in Baghdad that was at that point available to the outside world, these opening attacks created something of a fiery spectacle on American television screens, at least in the eyes of those untrained to distinguish among various images of bombings followed by fire. Indeed, many of the people who would

from that afternoon on be glued for days and days to their television sets believed that they were witnessing the opening of the unprecedentedly sensational air war that had been characterized beforehand as "shock and awe." This, it had been rumored, would be so potent and fearsome an assault from the air that it might cause the enemy to give up then and there, without resistance. Rumsfeld himself had remarked that the attack would "not be a repeat of any other conflict. It will be of a force and scope and scale beyond what has been seen before."

Yet no such attack took place, either on the first night or during the days to come. Here, then, was the first opportunity for the press to go after Rumsfeld. And it did, in spite of the fact that the ensuing air war was quite shocking and awesome enough in its own right.

THE UNITED States had, of course, gone to war against Iraq once before—in 1991, after Saddam Hussein invaded Kuwait and the George Bush who was then president declared, "This shall not stand." The first President Bush then put together a huge international coalition, and over a period of six months U.S. troops and materiel were dispatched to the neighborhood and amassed there in the desert of Saudi Arabia. Then, while eyes around the globe were glued on CNN (at that time the only channel broadcasting around-the-clock war coverage), American and British planes bombed Iraq mercilessly for forty-three days, after which U.S. ground forces took over, driving the Iraqis out of Kuwait and wreaking havoc on the regular Iraqi army. It was a rout, and on their retreat Iraqi soldiers were surrendering in droves—on at least one unforgettable occasion, even to an Italian journalist armed with nothing but a camera.

Whereupon the president called off the war—without bringing down Saddam Hussein or destroying his elite Republican Guard. Aside from the casualties the men in charge of the war feared that a move into Baghdad would cost, there was the UN resolution under whose aegis the war had been launched, and which authorized the operation solely for the limited purpose of reversing Saddam's invasion of Kuwait. Thus a cease fire was negotiated with the still unchastened (though possibly bewildered) Iraqi leader. It was the terms of this cease fire Saddam would systematically and barefacedly violate from that day until the evening of March 19, 2003.

This history would prove to be a significant factor in the course of the second Gulf war twelve years later. Having been allowed to remain in power in 1991, Saddam would soon after put down an uprising of the Shiites, who had been encouraged to rise and then abandoned by the Americans. He had put it down, moreover, with what was even for him a special measure of brutality. For this reason the Iraqi people in 2003 would place no stock in the American propaganda campaign that sought to enlist their cooperation in Saddam Hussein's defeat. In particular, the hoped-for uprisings by the once burned Shiites in southern Iraq never occurred. So, too, when Rumsfeld urged the Iraqi leaders to surrender in the early days of the war. For some at least, the memory of that betrayal still hung in the air. How could they be sure that Saddam would not survive a second time to wreak a terrible vengeance on them?

IT TOOK only about three weeks to convert Operation Iraqi Freedom from an ongoing battle into what had essentially become a mopping-up operation. By then it was clear that Saddam was gone, either dead, decamped to a neighboring country, or hiding somewhere underground. But on the other hand it was also

clear that the Americans would not be able to leave Iraq as quickly as certain policymakers seem to have expected. There was no king in exile, as there had been in the case of Afghanistan, for whom the people still retained some old feeling of loyalty and who could offer his blessings to a new government. Nor was there an obvious candidate to play the role being played by Hamid Karzai, someone who could begin early on to bring together at least the beginning elements of this new government. In short, Iraq socially, politically, and culturally was in a mess whose depth neither the war planners nor the diplomats seemed to have reckoned on. Except for the Baathist loyalists, most Iraqis were plainly relieved by Saddam's departure from the scene, but because they had been betrayed once before by the Americans, they made no secret of their suspicion that the coalition had come not to save but to exploit them in some way. This was not a climate in which it was going to be easy to bring them to the point of governing themselves.

To make matters worse, of all strains of Islam, Shiism was probably the one most antagonistic to the kind of cultural and political modernity represented by American society: It had, after all, been the capture of power by Shiism that had in 1979 turned Iran, a former faithful ally of the United States, into a bitter enemy.

In addition to cultural hostility and the memory of betrayal past, another factor came into play. Because the war plan called for the Americans to head directly northward from Kuwait to Baghdad, they did not stop to clean out the Baathist forces in the heavily Shiite southern cities. The result was that many of the Shiites there felt as if they were simply being left in the hands of their by-now possibly even more murderous oppressors. And finally there were the repeated American declarations—from

Allies: at 10 Downing Street with Tony Blair

Rumsfeld among others—that the United States was there to take down the regime and that what would replace it would be strictly up to the Iraqis. Instead of reassuring them that the "invaders" had no imperial designs either on their country or the potential wealth of their economy, at least some Iraqis took this to mean that they might once again be abandoned before they were in a condition to take control.

These suspicions and insecurities gradually began giving way to something more comforting to the Iraqis as well as more comfortable to the invading army. But they had nevertheless borne witness to the fact that the entity spoken of so often as "the Iraqi people" was a far more complicated one than certain enthusiasts for the war had contemplated.

ONE GREAT worry had, however, been averted: Saddam had not sabotaged Iraq's oil fields as he had Kuwait's in that earlier war; there would, then, be a plentiful source of wealth with which to rebuild the Iraqi economy.

Electricity was being restored, although where there would remain pockets of resistance—in Baghdad, in the predominantly Baathist towns where resistance would remain dangerous, or where the grids had for years been neglected and allowed to deteriorate into an almost irreparably primitive condition—it would remain sporadic. Still, food and clean water were being distributed among the population in ever greater quantities.[1]

---

[1] After fifty-five days, Commander-in-Chief Tommy Franks would be able to report that some Iraqis were indeed eating better than they had before the war.

A s A matter of policy great care had been taken during the fighting not to destroy too much of the country's infrastructure and to limit casualties among its civilian population (a policy that may well have cost the Americans and the British extra casualties of their own). Such care had been taken for various reasons. First, of course, there was the need to prove to the Iraqis that it was not they themselves but only the regime under which they had been forced to live that was the real and only target of the war. Second was the need to avoid conducting the war in a way that might destabilize any of Iraq's moderate Arab neighbors. "We couldn't know how long the war would last," says Rumsfeld, "and a long war with a lot of Al Jazeera videos and photographs of innocent Iraqi men, women, and children dying because of a less than discreet and precise bombing campaign could not only have the effect of killing innocent men, women, and children—which nobody with any sense wants to do— but it could also have had the effect of shaking up other countries." And finally, he points out, the people involved in planning the war hoped that by being discriminating about inflicting damage within Iraq, there would be a greater chance that the Iraqis might revolt against their government and thus both end the war quickly and make it possible for the country to be put back together under a new and benign government more quickly.

It did not happen as Franks and Rumsfeld and the others had hoped, of course, not only because a large number of the Iraqis remained suspicious of American intentions but also because the Iraqi underground known as the Fedayeen Saddam were simply killing people they suspected of going over to the enemy. Thus instead of rebelling, the soldiers who were able to do so were simply taking off their uniforms and slipping away.

A s FOR Donald Rumsfeld, during those same three weeks from the first bombardment to the taking of Baghdad he was subjected to what for some men might have been a whole career's worth of lows and highs, anxieties and satisfactions, about his role in shaping the conduct of the war.

In Iraq, somewhat sooner than he himself was fully prepared to do, Rumsfeld was called upon to act on his belief in a new, leaner, better integrated, more technologically sophisticated, twenty-first-century American military—to lay this belief on the line where it could be judged and its consequences measured. And it was indeed judged: almost immediately, at length, and, to put it mildly, in certain sectors of the press and the military far from tenderly. The difficulty was not mainly that the resentment and backbiting Rumsfeld had encountered in the Pentagon was now given a wide national airing in the form of various "expert" running comments on the war. This he could easily handle. What could not be easy to shoulder, for him as for anyone, was the responsibility for the real lives, most particularly the lives of American servicemen, that had been placed in his hands.

Rumsfeld had trained for war in the navy and had for long years remained in the naval reserve (until, as he once joked, as secretary of defense he had booted himself out). But the timing had been such that he had not actually been called upon to fight in a war: He was the member of that cohort that was too young for Korea and too old for Vietnam. Now others, young men and women—kids, really—would be fighting a war that he had had an important hand not only in bringing about but in planning for. This is, of course, the kind of responsibility normally given to generals and admirals, and not many civilians are ever asked to assume it.

Generals and admirals are known to deal with this burden by leaning heavily on precedent. As the old and rather unfeeling expression has it, they "always fight the last war." Rumsfeld, however, had no such recourse, precisely because he was refusing to fight the last war. This meant gambling on the belief he had developed in a new kind of military force and hence a new kind—or perhaps a better word for it is *style*—of warfare that would be fast, efficient, highly skilled, and that would integrate the particular arts and capabilities of the various services. This belief he then persuaded and/or required General Tommy Franks, the commander-in-chief in charge of Operation Iraqi Freedom (who had also been in charge of the war in Afghanistan) to put into action on the battlefield.

The plan for conducting a war against Iraq had been under consideration for some time, long before it became an immediate possibility. The issue of Iraq was in fact brought up several times in the course of the post-9/11 meetings between Bush and his national security team about what to do in Afghanistan. It was Rumsfeld's deputy, Paul Wolfowitz, who took the lead in trying to bring the discussion around to the need to do something about Iraq, as well. (Rumsfeld's commission on the ballistic missile threat had found that Iraq could actually pose such a threat to the United States in no more than ten years.) Later, during the planning stage of Operation Iraqi Freedom, Rumsfeld himself moved to the forefront, spending a great deal of time conferring with Tommy Franks about the right strategy.

The first thing Franks did was take the old plan for going up against Iraq off the shelf. However, everyone agreed, including Franks himself, that this plan was no longer relevant even as a starting point. "It was really ancient, years old," says Rumsfeld, "and didn't reflect the lessons we learned in Afghanistan. Nor did it reflect the current situation in Iraq, let alone the advance in American capability from dumb to smart bombs." There was no useful precedent to be found in the Gulf War of 1991—a war of vast forces that brought together some 430,000 American and

300,000 allied troops to pursue what turned out to be a highly re-
stricted objective. This time Rumsfeld wanted the lighter, faster,
and more mobile force he had long been contemplating. A good
deal of the success in Afghanistan had been achieved through the
use of special forces cooperating with local insurgents, and though
the situation in Iraq was different, Rumsfeld was thinking of a
force numbering not more than 125,000 to 130,000 troops—not all
of whom would be engaged in the actual fighting.

In the end, a compromise was reached between the "old" and
"new" warriors under which the number of troops would be
250,000.[2] Moreover, whereas in 1991 only a small proportion of the
munitions used had been precision-guided, by now approximately
80 percent of them would be. And, as in Afghanistan, greater use
would be made of special forces.

T HE WASHINGTON rumor mill that had for so long been
abuzz with accounts of tension and difficulty between
Rumsfeld and the military now had some seemingly fresh meat to
grind in the form of similar tales about the relation between
Rumsfeld and Tommy Franks. The story being circulated was that
the secretary demanded a light force, that Franks insisted on a
much heavier one, and that in the end both of them lost. Yet certain
senior military people who actually knew Franks said that he himself had always, since his days as an artillery commander, been an
innovative military thinker and that he, too, had long since come to

---

[2] Because one infantry division that was supposed to arrive in Iraq via Turkey was
finally forbidden to come onto Turkish soil and couldn't be brought into Iraq until the war was nearly over, for most of the time the number of American combatants probably came somewhat closer to what Rumsfeld had originally wanted.

appreciate the kind of warfare that involved joint operations by various branches of service. The truth was that he and Rumsfeld were on the same page, even if they disagreed over details. "Think of Rumsfeld as the composer and Franks as the orchestra leader," said Newt Gingrich, who knows both men, to the *Washington Post.*

Rumsfeld himself never ceased insisting that Franks had drawn up the war plan and that it had subsequently been accepted by everyone: the joint chiefs of staff in Washington, the combatant commanders around the world, and the National Security Council. From the opening day of a war, he says, the process of adjusting any war plan begins, because the combatants go to school on each other. (There must have been rather little going to school on the part of the Iraqi army, seeming largely to have been pretty much abandoned by its leaders after the start of this war and doing such things as running at American tanks with small trucks.) Something, for example, that is simply not knowable in advance, he points out, is how long it will take to unload a ship at a particular port. If it can be unloaded quickly, for instance, additional ships can be brought in. If not, they will have to wait. But essentially, he insists, the flow of coalition forces into Kuwait was determined by General Franks and John Handy of the U.S. Transportation Command back in January.

Rumsfeld also insists that the changes in the plan that needed to be improvised in response to conditions from day to day were also made by Franks. "I would be happy to take credit," he said, "but the reality is, the whole thing was worked out by the CINC."

After Operation Iraqi Freedom actually commenced, the old military adage that no war plan survives the first encounter with the enemy was cited by more than one of the myriad military experts who began to offer their expertise to the television audience. It was then repeated over and over for what seemed like days in explanation of what had obviously become a kind of war that no one—except perhaps those who had actually planned it—had expected. To begin with, there was the impressively quick change that resulted in the bombing of the compound in which Saddam Hussein was supposed to have been spending the evening. And then, in place of the much anticipated hours or days of airborne "shock and awe" came a steady stream of tanks, armored cars, and troops racing at record-breaking speed from the border of Kuwait to within fifty miles of Baghdad. All this filled the television screens to which everyone was glued, but well outside of camera range, special operations teams had been moving, as is their wont, under cover of darkness and secrecy into western Iraq, among other things to forestall the use of the country's western desert as a place from which to fire Scud missiles at Israel.

It seems likely, then, that a large part of the American public, which in 1991 had sat mesmerized for days and days at the spectacle of bombs pulverizing the Iraqi landscape, did not at first entirely understand the significance of the seemingly endless caravan of vehicles and men on dirt and debris-strewn highways. Moreover, puzzlement soon turned to anxiety as the airwaves and the pages of newspapers and magazines began to fill up with accounts of the war's—and Donald Rumsfeld's—dangerous shortcomings.

These accounts, with their attendant complaints against Rumsfeld's high-handedness, were already being put into circulation by *day three* of the war. Among the other shortcomings of which the public was repeatedly being reminded at this time was that none of Saddam Hussein's weapons of mass destruction—the ostensible reason for going after him in the first place—had yet been found. Could the whole enterprise, then, have been based on faulty intelligence? There were also many anxious questions about why Iraq's system of command and control had not yet been disrupted.

So much for day three of the war. On day four, retired Army General Barry McCaffrey—one of the authorities who would be offering regular comment throughout the progress of the conflict—declared, "Clearly [going to Baghdad] is going to be brutal, dangerous work and we could take, bluntly, a couple to three thousand casualties." "Clearly," in other words, he was reasoning as the generals in 1991 had reasoned about the likely result of making a move on Baghdad. On the following day McCaffrey told the *Washington Post* that "there should have been a minimum of two heavy divisions and an armored cavalry regiment on the ground—that's how our doctrine reads." At the same time, another retired military officer, Colonel Ralph Peters, who would continue saying "nay" until the very end and even well beyond victory, announced that Iraq would be liberated but this would happen despite serious strategic miscalculations. And according to Evan Thomas and John Barry of *Newsweek,* "Less than two weeks into the second gulf war" the idea that Operation Iraqi Freedom risked blowing up into a general Middle East war, "once very remote, [was] no longer unthinkable."

"Expert" analysis of this kind would open the way for many reporters and columnists who had been searching for a chance to give free play to their long-standing hostility to the Bush administration in general, and, no doubt for some of them, its secretary of defense in particular.[3]

One of the more nasty-intentioned accounts appeared in the *New Yorker* magazine, in a piece by Seymour Hersh entitled "Offense and Defense." Hersh had long been an assiduous hunter for crimes and misdemeanors committed by servants of the United States government. This time the hunt had taken him to the Pentagon, where, he declared, there was a great deal of anger at the

---

[3] None of them surpassed the *New York Times* columnist Maureen Dowd. Her bile where Rumsfeld was concerned quickly succeeded in upending what had in previous years passed for wit but had now, with Republicans in power, become nothing more than out-of-control vituperation.

way Rumsfeld and his inner circle of advisers had insisted on mi-
cromanaging the war. " 'He thought he knew better,' " someone
identified as a "senior planner" told Hersh. This "planner" then
went on to describe how Rumsfeld had " 'further stunned the joint
staff by insisting that he would control the timing and flow of army
and marine troops to the combat zone.' " In addition, there were
the dozen or so informants whom Hersh identified merely as
"people I had spoken to." According to these "people," Rumsfeld
had "simply failed to anticipate the consequences of protracted
warfare." Moreover, they pointed out, supply lines—"inevitably"—
had become overextended and vulnerable to attack. In fact, they
said, during the week that had just passed, shortages had forced
Central Command to "run around looking for supplies." One also
conveniently unnamed but, according to Hersh, "senior" administration official had commented to him about the Iraqis, " 'Ain't it
something? They're not scared.' "

The decision to go directly to Baghdad—leaving the battle for
each of the Baath-controlled cities on the way to forces coming on
later—was another issue about which the critics expressed deep
worry. And when the progress northward was temporarily stopped
by a raging sandstorm, the alarms grew even louder, as if the war
planners should somehow have provided in advance for the fact
that nature itself might for a day or two be against them. To top it
off, there had at one point been a mix-up in the delivery of supplies, undoubtedly the very mix-up that Hersh's unnamed informants had so darkly characterized as a "shortage." But what had
actually happened was that the columns had moved so fast, some of
the troops were left without enough food for a day. The pleasure of
the outrage expressed about this in certain of the nation's news-
rooms was palpable.

For a while, then, it felt as if the only cheering thoughts about
the war were to be found in the reports of journalists who were

"embedded" with the troops and were thus privy to what was actually happening, in the daily briefings from Central Command in Doha, Qatar, and in pictures like that of Baghdadis dancing on the toppled and broken statue of Saddam Hussein.

And the secretary himself? He soldiered on, with a confident calm that few men could have sustained under so fierce a barrage of hostility, and only now and then, and again mostly for effect, expressing any notable irritation. (However, General Richard Myers did positively explode one afternoon during a joint briefing with Rumsfeld. In a great fit of unpracticed temper he answered a question about the reports that the war was going badly by declaring them most emphatically to be "bogus," "false," and "absolutely wrong." "There may be others," he went on at some length and at white heat, "that have other ideas of how we should have done it . . . God bless them, that's a great sport here inside the Beltway. . . . " And more in this vein. So surprising was this display on the part of the normally businesslike and good-humored general, especially by contrast with Rumsfeld's own quiet and careful description of the progress of the war, that the following day the story of Myers's explosion was front-page news.)

This particular briefing took place on April 1. By the middle of the month—only *three weeks* after the war had begun—it was effectively over. What remained for the coalition forces to do was something that would prove in its way more difficult and dangerous but could not be called war: namely, to reestablish some degree of order in the midst of chaos, disorder, criminality, and guerrillas (a word the authorities for some reason refuse to use) disguised as unhappy citizens. After so many years of Saddamite murder, oppression, and torture, bringing order to Iraq was a process that would at first be reckoned in terms of at least many months but has more recently come to be recognized as a matter of years. In any case, it was not something to be reckoned in numbers of days. But days seemed by then to have become the standard unit of time for measuring progress.

Not that the old critics of the war plan were silenced by its spectacular success. On the contrary: They now went looking for defeat in the jaws of victory. One of the more interesting examples was a postmortem on the war by Ralph Peters. In analyzing what had gone right and what, more to the point, had gone wrong, Peters began with "the shock-and-awe air campaign," which, he wrote, "was such a disappointment that Pentagon briefers immediately wrote it out of the war's history, much the way Stalin's Politburo used to erase purged figures from official photographs." The second thing to go wrong, in Peters's view, was "the ideologically motivated refusal to send more troops to the theater of war prior to hostilities. When commanders in combat complained that they needed more troops, senior leaders silenced them. . . . Certainly we won a magnificent victory. But our military won it *despite* the [office of the secretary of defense]'s micromanagement. . . . This has been a brilliant campaign," he finally conceded. "But it was won by soldiers, not by civilian experts who regard our troops as nothing more than strategic janitors." Then, for the final out-of-control sting in the tail, "The recent suggestions by party hacks who disdained military service to the effect that they and their ideas won the war is conduct unbecoming. Even by Washington's standards." Who these "hacks" might be was left to Peters's readers to decide. In any case, they could not even by a minimal standard of decency have included the secretary himself.

Ugly as this was, the prize for flat-out nastiness went to Michelle Cottle of the *New Republic*. "It's not just that Rumsfeld is pleased about the way the war went," she remarked. "(Hell, we're all pleased about that.) It's more that, high on the fumes of military victory, the secretary seems to have decided that he is, in fact, a military and foreign affairs genius who no longer needs to suffer any criticism, or even mild disagreement, from mere mortals." After a good deal more in this vein, including mention of a classified memo allegedly circulated by Rumsfeld and leaked to the *New York Times* that called for an immediate regime change in North Korea, Cottle observed, "The defense secretary . . . seems to regard his battlefield successes as proof that his long-held worldview—diplomacy is for losers—should now dominate administration policy. . . . At any rate, any day now you expect a power-crazed Rumsfeld to crown himself Caesar and lead his troops in an assault on Foggy Bottom. With those wussbags at State out of the picture, surely President Bush could be made to see that Rummy's way is the only way to run a great empire. Then, on to France!" (*Donald Rumsfeld?* Circulating a classified memo? That would be the day. Miss Cottle's editor was no doubt unable to curb her enthusiasm.)

It seems evident that in spreading gloom the "experts" were not expressing anxiety that the United States might lose the war—that had been out of the question from the first moment. Rather what they appeared to be doing was taking this opportunity to settle old scores. As for the journalists who became the willing participants in their campaign, some of them were no doubt merely floating along on the tide of the opinion of others, but a number of them were also engaged in settling scores: either with George Bush for being president, or, like the *New York Times's* R. W. Apple, over a war they believed the United States should never have got itself into, or, in a few all-too-familiar cases, with the United States of America itself.

F OR ALL his calm when under attack, Rumsfeld at one point began to look rather grim. The lines on his face seemed to have grown deeper and his color, never all that vivid, seemed to have become grayer. When asked whether this was the result of all the public attacks on him and on the war he was overseeing, Joyce Rumsfeld answered, "Oh, no. The truth is, he had decided that he was too heavy and needed to lose some weight. The look you are talking about is what happens to someone whose loss of weight becomes visible in his face first."

Put himself on a diet at such a time? It was a reminder of the self-discipline shown by the would-be congressman who hired himself a speech teacher; by the head of Searle who refused to answer a last-minute question from the representative of the Monsanto company minutes before the deal between them was to go through; and by the secretary of defense who had stood his ground at the risk of incurring the enmity of many senior members of the government agency he had been appointed to oversee. Anyone who thought, or even merely hoped, to see Donald Rumsfeld vanquished and relieved of his responsibilities was well advised to think again.

In any case, in early April, when hostility to him in the press was at its most intense, a Gallup poll found that 71 percent of the people polled (89 percent of Republicans) approved of the job Rumsfeld was doing, and 65 percent thought that his involvement in the military planning for the war had been "helpful"—Gallup's word—to the U.S. efforts in Iraq. Poll numbers rarely go higher than that. So much for the vaunted power of the press.

THREE WEEKS into the war the secretary was asked whether the "Rumsfeld doctrine" had replaced the "Powell doctrine" (meaning the doctrine that prescribed a vast army and weeks of preliminary bombing for the Gulf War). "I wouldn't call it the 'Rumsfeld doctrine,'" he answered. "It's the law of physics. Which is to say, in this case speed was more important than mass. What was done by starting the ground war rather than engaging in the kind of long air war of 1991 was that General Franks and his team avoided killing an enormous number of innocent people and inflicting a lot of collateral damage. We did not have strategic surprise, but we gained tactical surprise by starting on the ground—everyone was expecting an air war. No one believed we would start the war without the 4th Infantry Division, which was still in the Mediterranean, hoping to come through Turkey. The effect was that the oil fields were not burned, there are no masses of refugees, no masses of internally displaced people, no massive collateral damage, and neighboring countries were not hit with Scuds. So I think that when this is over, speed will be seen as having achieved a great deal."

Troubles would lie ahead, but they would be the troubles, in fact, of victory. And in the end who could honestly doubt the brilliance of the military plan—which Rumsfeld would continue to insist (and everyone else refuse to believe) was Tommy Franks's alone?

9

STORMY WEATHER

V ICE PRESIDENT Cheney was in his office musing on Operation Iraqi Freedom in the company of two reporters from the *New York Times,* John H. Cushman Jr. and Thom Shanker. The date was April 9, which happened to be the day that witnessed the fall of Baghdad. And though senior Pentagon officials had warned that there would be tough fighting ahead, the reporters noted, "they could not disguise their glee at the way things were playing out." Cheney was comparing this war to the 1991 Persian Gulf War, during which he himself had been secretary of defense. In that war, he said, only one combat aircraft in five could have dropped a bomb on a target sighted by a laser; now they all could. Furthermore, he said, fewer

Addressing U.S. troops at Al Udeid Air Base, Qatar: Their troubles would be the troubles of victory. . . .

than 10 percent of the weapons dropped then were precision-guided; this time the percentage was 68. In that war a strike might happen two days after a reconnaissance plane photographed a target; now it could be made in virtually an instant. Finally, commanders then depended on such low technology as maps, grease pencils, and radios; now, even in a combat vehicle, one could click a mouse and see the war unfold on video displays. But the biggest difference of all, Cheney said, was not the technological advances made since 1991 but rather that technology had enabled planners to engage in an entirely new way of thinking about the conduct of warfare.

Without intending to, the vice president here provided the explanation for at least some of the opposition to the conduct of the war, namely, its unexpectedness. The whole thing, after all, would ultimately take only six weeks, from the first night of bombing to the official announcement, three weeks after the fall of Baghdad, that the military phase of Operation Iraqi Freedom was now finished. Which is, to understate the case, not bad—especially considering both the size and condition of Iraq. In 1991's Desert Storm, the pre-ground-war bombing alone had gone on for six weeks.

Yet almost from the first minute, in the papers and magazines as well as on the air, the American public was treated to expressions of anxiety and even dire warnings about how the war was going. Assuming that at least some of the people who sounded these alarms did so disinterestedly—that is, not because they resented Rumsfeld's treatment of the army, or his much alleged stubbornness and/or arrogance, or even merely Bush's presence in the White House, but because they honestly feared that the operation as it had been planned was questionable—would that not have been an odd fear to announce to the world after only three or four days? Would it not have been especially odd for someone with military experience? Yet that is precisely what happened.[1] Again, as-suming that in at least a few cases there were no extraneous per-sonal motives, how is it to be accounted for?

One of the problems, as the columnist Charles Krauthammer pointed out, was that the intention to go to war had until the very last minute been left in the clouds: Would we or wouldn't we go into Iraq? There was a promise in the air—a promise produced in good faith but perhaps with some malicious effect—that the threat of war itself might bring about a change of regime in Iraq. When it did not and the war then began, some people were bewildered. They had been given the impression that the war would be easy (a "cakewalk," in Kenneth Adelman's phrase), that it would be over, almost literally, in a flash. Rumsfeld himself had been understood to say something like this when he predicted that the war would be unlike any ever seen. Why, then, was so much of Iraq being left in-tact and in a condition to offer menace of various kinds to our troops? In other words, it was the very unfamiliarity of the Rumsfeld-Franks way of conducting war that aroused anxiety.

To be sure, though he was indeed hit with a barrage of criticism about the way the war was being fought—much of it pointing not so much to supposed errors in his thinking as to shortcomings in his character and personality—Rumsfeld had by no means been

---

[1] Moreover, as late as mid-May—the issue now being the postwar reconstruction of Iraqi society—Ralph Peters complained that there were still not enough troops in Iraq to do what was necessary. They might have won the war handily (which in his view, however, had nothing to do with the war plan and was only the result of the quality of the armed forces), but now there were not enough boots on the ground to establish the rule of law. And why? Because Rumsfeld had "sought to minimize the role of ground forces in order to justify cutting the army and fun-neling the savings to defense contractors." This last piece of nastiness was a new allegation, reminiscent of nothing so much as the classic moment in a 1950s movie when someone turns to the embittered heroine and says, "He must have hurt you terribly."

left undefended, by either columnists and commentators or members of the military. Typical among the supporters of the way Operation Iraqi Freedom was being fought, as well as of Rumsfeld's role in it, was a member of the faculty of the Naval War College named Mackubin Owens. Halfway through the war (which itself seems an odd thing to say about a piece published in the second week of fighting) Owens analyzed the complaints of both the army officers who charged that Rumsfeld wanted to gut ground forces in favor of air power and the air-power advocates who complained that too many targets had been placed off-limits. The problem with both of these views, said Owens, is that they looked at warfare as something apart from politics, which it could never be—and most of all in a struggle whose aim was to liberate a people from their oppressive rulers.

Another defense on similar grounds came from Lawrence Kaplan of the *New Republic* and was echoed in a number of places elsewhere. "[F]ew of [the] critics bothered to entertain a simpler and legitimate rationale for the war plan, namely, that it was drawn up with an eye toward political as well as military goals."

True, Iraq's weapons of mass destruction and Saddam's connections with terrorism had dominated the prewar argument for going into Iraq, but in the end these issues could not be separated from a vision of bringing about the creation of a peaceable and politically decent regime in the midst of a dangerously turbulent region. At the very beginning of the military operation it was Rumsfeld himself who had spoken not of finding and destroying WMDs but of ridding the Iraqi people of a murderous regime.

Now, in the long history of world affairs, such an aim would undoubtedly have to be seen as a peculiarly American rationale for threatening or going to war—a rationale, moreover, that has served more than once to rally the country's voters: that is, neither for territory nor for economic gain nor, in the strictest meaning of the term, for defense of the homeland, but rather to rid the world of a noxious regime that is also a danger to others, its own people especially, as well as to ourselves. Aside from Rumsfeld's having characterized them as "old," one of the things that may have stirred the juices of resentment among the Western Europeans was just this: The appeal for so many Americans in the idea that their country has a uniquely beneficent role to play in the world. Nevertheless it is the case that if American technology had made it possible to fight such a war, and fear of both terrorism and Saddam Hussein's intentions had made it seem urgent to do so, decades and decades of

Introducing singer-songwriter Darryl Worley before his concert in the center courtyard of the Pentagon

high American hopes for the world had also gone into shaping the war's aims.

RUMSFELD BELIEVES that the criticism of the war leveled inside, or in the neighborhood of, the Pentagon had almost certainly originated among people who were unaware of the general shape as well as the details of the war plan. For, he points out, since the major occupation of those who work for the Defense Department is organizing, equipping, and training the armed forces, only a modest number of people in that building could have been really familiar with the plan. The responsibility for planning wars, he insists, remains in the hands of the combatant commanders headquartered around the world.

Some time around mid-April—in the face of what could no longer be denied had been a quick and brilliant victory—the tide of negative comment about the conduct of the war began to subside. In Western Europe, and on the literary Left in Britain, the success in Iraq seemed if anything to increase the ardor of anti-American sentiment, but on this side of the Atlantic, the steady stream of carping against the operation now came mainly from those who had been, and who would remain, opposed to the war in the first place. The opposition of such people, particularly the literary and show business celebrities among them, could hardly be assuaged by victory, and thus they continued on their accustomed rounds, their influence (such as it was) largely spent. As for the military pundits who had been crying doom, they may or may not have been embarrassed by their predictions of failure and massive casualties, but in any case they were no longer all that much in evidence.

The historian Walter A. McDougall summed up what now appeared to be the general sentiment: "Never have offensive military operations achieved so much, so quickly, so far away, and so cheaply in terms of both casualties and money. Shock and awe? Those most shocked and in awe are the American politicians and pundits who warned of bloodbaths, quagmires, lost legions, and bridges too far."

However, one issue remained that was bound to bedevil the Bush administration for the foreseeable future, and that was the fact that after some time and effort put in to searching for them, no WMDs were being turned up. According to the polls, the other crimes and horrors unearthed in Iraq—weapons stashed in schools and hospitals, torture chambers, mass graves (somehow made all the more horrible by their juxtaposition with Saddam's numerous and almost unbelievably richly-appointed palaces)—were regarded by the general public as adequate justification for the war. But not by critics of the war, and not even by some supporters who now threatened to turn retroactively against it. Even before the search was anything near being over, most people concluded either that Saddam Hussein had destroyed the WMDs on the eve of the war or had moved them to the territory of some neighboring ally, perhaps Syria.

By the summer preparations would be actively under way for the following year's presidential campaign, which gave Bush's Democratic opponents a powerful incentive to keep the issue of the absent WMDs alive. If the war had been a success, at least its rationale could now be claimed to have been false and, worse than false, a lie told on the basis of deliberately manipulated intelligence reports.

O N THE same day that Baghdad fell and Cheney was ruminating about the war, Rumsfeld made a journey across town to appear before the House of Representatives. Because of his struggles with the army brass and certain other problems, he could not necessarily be sure that he would find a friendly welcome in the House. This time, however, he was greeted with a standing ovation. As a result, it began to cross his mind that in some not too distant future the applause for this new kind of warfare might be parlayed into congressional cooperation with his efforts to make the military both a more efficient and a more benign profession.

It was now also widely remarked that Rumsfeld's triumph was to be chalked up as a defeat for Colin Powell. Almost from the beginning of George W. Bush's administration, the inside Washington betting line on the two secretaries had been that they were playing a zero-sum game, in which one could not win without the other's losing. So, for instance, very few defenders of Rumsfeld's role in planning the war failed to mention that a vast number of American troops (along with many others) had been amassed for then-General Colin Powell's Iraq war to achieve a tragically minimal purpose. Then, in early May, it was announced that retired General Jay Garner, who had arrived in Iraq to oversee the postwar transition and very quickly appeared to be the wrong man for this most complicated of jobs, was being replaced.[2] The man named to replace him was L. Paul Bremer, a former foreign-service officer who had, among other things, served as ambassador to the Netherlands and who later, on leaving government, became a member of Kissinger Associates. Instantly—and, as it would turn out, mistakenly—the Washington gossip mill declared Bremer's appointment a victory for the State Department over the Pentagon. What the appointment did bespeak, however, was the recognition that taking control of Iraq was going to be a longer and more complicated task than the war planners had once clearly hoped.

---

[2] Typically, Rumsfeld denies this and says that Garner had intended to be in Iraq for only a short time.

Of course, given how fundamental the differences are between the mind-set behind the processes of diplomacy and that behind a commitment to military power, some degree of conflict between State and Defense is inevitable no matter who their respective secretaries may be. But with regard to Rumsfeld-Powell, the conflict was usually represented by "insider" journalism as more personal than institutional. Thus, when in September 2002 the president went to the UN to appeal for international support on Iraq, his decision to do so was alleged to be a victory for Powell and a defeat for Rumsfeld and his gang of hawks in the Defense Department. By the same token, when the UN Security Council refused Bush's request, the pundits listed the refusal in Powell's defeat column, and when Operation Iraqi Freedom got under way, it was accounted a win for Rumsfeld.

This is a game that, while others are eager to play it for him, Rumsfeld predictably refuses to join. Others are also clearly eager to play the game on Powell's behalf: Numerous unpleasant remarks about Rumsfeld and his conduct have issued from various "anonymous sources" at the State Department. Rumsfeld, however, insists that he and Powell have been friendly since the days of his first tour at the Pentagon, when Powell was only a colonel. (Indeed, he has a picture of himself with the young Powell hanging in his office and leads people who inquire about the much advertised tensions between the two men to it.) "We have a good personal relationship and a very good professional relationship. We speak together every morning and are physically together probably an average of once a day. He is in an institution that has certain statutory responsibilities," says Rumsfeld with the formality that this issue invariably brings out in him, "and I am in an institution that has certain statutory responsibilities. He has his own personal views about the world, and I have mine. The main thing," he continues, "is that we both work for a president who is a very strong leader. Whenever a certain kind of decision is made, people say that it was Powell's, or that it was mine. The fact is, it is the president who decides. And this president, make no mistake about it, is a very decisive man."

But questions of personal relations aside, as the historian Victor Davis Hanson pointed out, Rumsfeld's accomplishments have likely provided Powell with "more diplomatic leverage than any secretary of state in recent memory precisely because the new military can move so rapidly and unexpectedly with lethal power—a fact that will bring [Powell] a host of obsequious foreign visitors." (It is interesting to note that two of the English-speaking world's most widely admired writers on military affairs, John Keegan and Victor Davis Hanson, make a great point of characterizing Rumsfeld as a radical. This is an idea about him that clearly intrigues, and seems not in the least to disturb, him.)

WHERE POSTWAR Iraq was concerned, if reporters and commentators had been surprised by the way the war was fought, they were even more unprepared for what was taking place in its aftermath. For what seems to have been left out of many people's calculations was the possibility that American troops might encounter widespread looting, lawlessness, and pockets of underground resistance. These possibilities seem also to have been left out of the calculations of the war planners themselves, whose repeated denials that the United States intended to remain as an occupying army in Iraq for very long may have had an effect opposite to the one intended. Instead, that is, of providing reassurance, these denials may well have added to the Iraqis' feelings of insecurity and resentment. Anyway, as scenes of looting[3] and shooting and Imams calling for demonstrations against the Americans were being reported and transmitted via television, new anxieties arose: Would this prove to be a quagmire after all?

In other words, having been vindicated about the efficacy of the war plan, Rumsfeld was now being challenged on the issue of conditions in postwar Iraq. In view of the fact that our troops were still being fired on, and some of them killed, was the war in fact over? What was being done about casual violence and theft? Why had the coalition been so slow in restoring electricity? Why were the efforts of the relief agencies that had come into Iraq so chaotic?

In press conference after press conference Rumsfeld now pointed out that the very speed of the war had left these problems to be dealt with later; the main thing had been to get to Baghdad and take down the regime. Moreover, he would add, in the days just before the war started, Saddam Hussein had opened the prisons and dumped back into the population anywhere from fifty thousand to one hundred thousand prisoners who were now on the loose. It would take time to find them and figure out how to deal with them. There were still Baathist loyalists out to make mischief, along with members of the Republican Guard and the underground Fedayeen Saddam, now acting as guerrillas and snipers. There were also members of the Iranian National Guard and others from nearby countries who had come across the border into Iraq in order to add to the mischief. As for the WMDs, it was possible that they had been destroyed before the coalition moved in;

---

[3] It is interesting that amid all the expressed outrage over the looting, no one saw fit to mention that looting has historically been done by the soldiers of invading armies, not by the local populace. In this case, all too ironically, the Americans were being upbraided not for being rapacious but for failing to stop the Iraqis from being so.

on the other hand, it was also possible that they would yet be found: There were knowledgeable informants who swore that the weapons were still in the country. We just don't know, he would say over and over, we just don't know. As we also do not know what had happened either to Saddam Hussein or to his sons.

"What we do know about Saddam, however," Rumsfeld would conclude emphatically, "is that he is no longer running Iraq."

The main center of the lawlessness seemed to be Baghdad, a city of five and a half million—though it would not take long for incidents of disorder, and the wounding and killing of American and British troops, to crop up from day to day in a variety of other cities, particularly in the Baath dominated areas to the north and west.

During a call-in radio program on which he had agreed to be a guest, the secretary was asked if he was happy with the way things were going in Baghdad. "I am never satisfied, nobody is," he answered. "But if you look at the number of murders in American cities, along with the numbers of robberies and larcenies and burglaries, and you compare them, for instance, with the size of Baghdad . . . it's pretty clear that in the cities of the world in general there is something other than perfect order. . . ."

Just how long the United States would have to stay in Iraq, and just how large the contingent remaining there would have to be, were questions that Rumsfeld did not attempt to answer. (As time wore on, of course, it began to be apparent that bringing order to that unhappy country would take a good deal longer, and possibly involve more troops, than anyone had counted on or prepared for.) Meanwhile, Ambassador Bremer was working hard to subdue the lawlessness and to engage Iraqis in the process of returning some modicum of order to their country.

Just as he is not willing to speculate about how long American forces may have to remain in Iraq, he also refuses to guess at what else might happen in the region as a result of the American victory. Questions regarding the future of American policy, he unbudgingly insists, are for the president alone to answer.

B UT, ESPECIALLY with the main military aspect of the Iraqi operation over, there remained what Rumsfeld referred to as the "statutory responsibilities" of the institution he had been appointed to run. If you want me to change it, I'll change it, Rumsfeld had said to the president about "the building." Now despite Rumsfeld's own insistence that the war plan had not been his but General Franks's, the fact was that the operation in Iraq had vindicated his thinking about a new kind of military. And then some. In other words, he was now in a strong position to fulfill the offer he had made to the president more than two wars ago.

Somewhere around the middle of April Rumsfeld requested Congress to grant him broad new powers that would enable him to reshape the armed forces from top to bottom. He wanted, for example, to be able to extend the tenure of generals and admirals serving in particularly important jobs and at the same time to ease the way into retirement of those unlikely to be promoted any further. He also wanted to be able to transfer some three hundred thousand military support jobs to civilian employees, which would increase the number of troops available for combat without having to add to the size of the uniformed force. He requested a change in regulations that would enable military personnel for whom full-time service had become temporarily difficult to switch from active duty to the reserves, and then later allow them to return to active duty again. Retirement age for the most senior generals and admirals, he said, should be raised beyond sixty-two, and service in certain four-star positions should be extended beyond the present single term. In addition, people in the armed services tended to be moved from job to job after two years or less, so they were not really around in any job long enough to learn from their mistakes. "They spend the first six months saying hello to everybody, the next six months trying to learn the job, and the last six months leaving," Rumsfeld argues. "I like people to be in a job long enough to make mistakes and clean them up before they go on to make mistakes somewhere else."

During the following month he testified before the Defense Subcommittee of the Senate Appropriations Committee, requesting for 2003 a $48 billion increase over the defense budget for the preceding year. The country was now being called upon to accomplish three difficult missions at once, he explained: to fight the global war on terrorism; to catch up on investments that were delayed during what he termed "the procurement holiday of the last decade"; and to prepare for wars in the future by transforming our military into a force suited to conditions in the twenty-first century. All three of these things must be done simultaneously, he continued. We cannot put off transforming the armed forces while we fight the war on terrorism, for as we learned to our sorrow on September 11, our adversaries have been busily engaging in transformations of their own.

If Congress were to approve, remarked David S. C. Chu, under secretary of defense for personnel and readiness, all this would mark the biggest reorganization of military personnel in half a century.

If Congress were to approve: There was the rub. "As I keep saying, the Congress is Article I of the Constitution. And they know it, and they should," says Rumsfeld. "They have an important responsibility—all legislative power, appropriations, control of the purse strings, oversight. Now, the executive branch has its own set of responsibilities, and to fulfill ours becomes ever more difficult, because of the committee structure of the Congress along with the fact that the executive branch is organized in a way that was arrived at incrementally over many, many decades during the industrial age and is hard to change. The committee structure of Congress was made to fit this kind of organization, and its members control the purse strings for the various departments and agencies. The difficulty is that in the information age the problems that need to be dealt with don't fit neatly into the old industrial-age arrangement. And so it takes an enormous amount of interagency work just to try to make sense of a problem and to get everyone who has some statutory responsibility for it involved in dealing with the problem—in other words, to get a whole bunch of threads up through the eye of the needle."

"You can, of course," he concludes, "always avoid the inevitable tension produced in this arrangement by doing nothing. You can avoid it by saying that everything is fine. You can avoid it by acquiescing in anything that anyone else thinks is appropriate. That way, of course, you end up having a very pleasant tour of duty. But as for me," he adds, laughing, "I was having a very pleasant life before I got here, so I didn't come looking for a pleasant tour of duty. I came thinking, maybe we can do some good, get some things changed. And once you start down that road, of course, somebody's not going to like it."

Whoever that somebody, or those somebodies, might now turn out to be was not necessarily predictable. What was predictable, however, is that there would continue to be conflict in Rumsfeld's life as secretary of defense—whether about the development of this or that weapon, the making of this or that appointment, or the implementation of this or that change in personnel practice. What was equally predictable was that anyone who opposed him would soon discover, as many already had, that he could simultaneously be both an immovable object and an irresistible force.

10

"... A Man Who Danced with His Wife"

H E HAD been having a very pleasant life before he came to Washington this time, he said. And indeed he had. From a certain point of view his life might even have seemed an ideal mix: some business activity, some important service to the nation, some local civic responsibility, and time left over to spend with children, grandchildren, and good friends in his beloved New Mexico. In addition, he had been heaped with honors—medals, awards, honorary doctorates almost too numerous to keep track of. A man approaching his seventieth year might have taken a great deal of satisfaction in a whole lot less.

With General Tommy Franks: The plan for the war, according to Rumsfeld, was all his.

Joyce, too, was now settled comfortably—and, as she mistakenly thought, permanently. (Her father, once famous far and wide for being cheerful and refusing to say anything bad about anyone, had a number of years earlier suffered a debilitating stroke, and after being lovingly tended by his wife until she could no longer manage, died in a nursing home. Recently it had become her mother's turn to need nursing-home care, and she would die in early February of 2003.) The Rumsfeld children were now grown and somewhat scattered—Marcy lived in Chicago but Valerie was in Santa Fe, and Nicholas, in Portland, Oregon. From her empty nest Joyce had been pouring her considerable energies into creating and managing a foundation devoted to improving Chicago's schools, an issue that had long engaged her and that under somewhat different circumstances, and in their respective settings, would engage her daughters as well. And she would continue to busy herself, as always, with the care and feeding of a voluminous and almost uniquely close-held circle of friendships—an art that she has carried to its highest point.

Still, in the Rumsfeld household there was clearly energy left to burn. Just as clearly, Don would not have made the move to Washington were he not intending to leave some kind of indelible mark on the place from which he had returned home to the Midwest twenty-four years earlier.

He understood from the outset that any attempt to reassert civilian control over the Pentagon would involve him in some kind of battle. And not having fallen out of touch with Washington— among other things there were those jobs he did for Reagan and later, there were the two congressional commissions on which he served as chairman—he also anticipated just how heated such a battle might turn out to be. (On the other side, anyone acquainted with the course of his career in business during the intervening years would not have been surprised to learn that his cool would ultimately best the joint staff's heat.)

Two things, however, he could not really have imagined. The first was that within two years of his return to the Pentagon he would be engaged in the planning of not just one but two wars. Especially in the case of Iraq, this meant that he would have to push for—or, if the plan for Operation Iraqi Freedom was really General Tommy Franks's baby, would have to encourage—a style of warfare that certain members of the military, active and retired, would find too revolutionary to accept. Push for—or encourage—and then wait in a state of at least reasonable calm and at least the appearance of good cheer to be vindicated.

Another thing he could not have imagined—it would prove to be not a negligible one—was that in addition to taking on the Department of Defense, what also awaited him was an entirely different second career: that of national, and even international, celebrity. "In Washington," says his friend Muggy Hoffman, the wife of Princeton classmate and former Secretary of the Army Martin Hoffman, "to be anywhere he is has become chic. People actually follow him around. There was even a story in the newspaper one day about his having been out to dinner with some friends the night before, including an account of what he ate and how much he tipped."

When asked about this other new role, Rumsfeld sometimes laughs and sometimes shrugs, in either case with ever so slight an edge of irritability. It appears that neither New Trier High School (though stars of stage and screen were among its many distinguished graduates) nor Princeton nor the navy nor the Congress nor, certainly, Chicago's business world had provided him with that special lightness of touch that enables celebrities to be at ease in the face of displays of heated admiration from casual passersby.

No man, no matter how serious of purpose or how suspicious of popular opinion, could be indifferent to the experience of having been designated, as Rumsfeld was, one of the world's sexiest men. The only question is what he allows himself to make of it.

Rumsfeld appears not to have decided on the answer. Perhaps he hears his Midwestern mother cautioning him, as so many Midwestern mothers used to caution their sons, not to become "conceited." Or perhaps he considers dealing with this phenomenon a waste of what, in the course of his usual eighteen-hour workdays, would be an all-too-precious amount of time. What is certain is that he either does not really, or does not permit himself to, take the measure of what this newfound figuredom means.

The experience that comes to Donald Rumsfeld most naturally is that of power and the things that go with it—whether the power of a government, of an army, of a large corporation, or, for that matter, of a mountain. He tends, for example, almost by his very nature to probe those around him for weaknesses, toward which, should he find them, he might not necessarily be tender. On the other hand, when he meets his match, whether in seriousness of intellect, clear-headedness, courage, or perhaps even just in sheer will, he is ready to engage with gusto.

Now, power may or may not be an aphrodisiac, as Henry Kissinger once famously observed. But one thing is sure: Power is in an important sense the very opposite of celebrity. People who are powerful usually have a superior hold on those who are weaker than they are. Celebrities, however, willy-nilly become the almost wholly-owned property of those who celebrate them. Watch a movie star who wishes to be left alone walk down a city street or into a restaurant and note the lengths of disguise to which he or she will go in order to avoid having the walk or the meal simply, and by right, taken over by fans.

The distinction between being powerful and being a star is not

unimportant, and especially not unimportant for thinking about this latest phase in Rumsfeld's long and various career. He has in the course of his life never wanted for approval or admiration, whether as a student, in the navy, in the government, or in business. How else, to take just one example, would someone lacking even one day's experience in the field simply be handed a large and floundering pharmaceutical company to run? Nor has Rumsfeld ever, not even from his very first months in Congress, appeared to encounter difficulty with, or shown hesitation about, asserting his claim to authority. But place him in a roomful of people crowding around to shake his hand and sing his praises, and unless they are, say, members of the armed forces, civilian employees of the Pentagon, or hangers-out at Capitol Hill and other familiar haunts—that is, people whose reasons for admiration and enthusiasm are transparent to him—he becomes visibly less than comfortable.

Be that as it may, there is something in the phenomenon of Rumsfeld's extraordinary celebrity that speaks as much to the present and future condition of the United States as to his own ongoing career. And that is the fact that his status seems to transcend partisan politics. For among the men and women who have in one way or another declared themselves members of the Donald Rumsfeld fan club[1] there are believing liberals as well as conservatives and otherwise loyal Democrats as well as Republicans. His female admirers are especially relevant in this connection because for years the public opinion polls have shown that women tend on the whole to be more anti-military than men.

After 9/11, of course, the map of that once so vividly divided red-and-blue country lost something of its sharp outlines, so that

---

[1] Yes, there is such a thing, figuratively if not literally, attested to by the existence of at least two Websites exclusively devoted to keeping track of his triumphs.

by November of 2002 Bush was able to parlay what had been a virtual tie for the presidency into an almost unprecedented midterm victory for his party. In addition, despite the later efforts of a number of pundits and politicians to persuade their fellow Americans that the aftermath of the Iraq war was turning out to be a murderous disappointment if not indeed evidence of outright government deception, a very large percentage of Americans have continued to favor Bush with their approval. One thing that Rumsfeld can be said to have in common with Bush, in fact, is the way that they both continue to cut a more than usually wide swath of admiration with the public.

Obviously, in many respects the two men could hardly be more unlike. Although they are both men who know their own minds and understand to the very bottom of their beings what is involved in the exercise of will, in matters of personal style they bear almost no resemblance to one another. Bush is famously a tease and a kibitzer, the kind of man who, as the Good Book might have said, turneth away wrath with a well-timed neighborly slap on the back. Whereas Rumsfeld is, first, last, and always, a contender. And when it comes to the question of dealing with the problem of one's all-too-human inner weaknesses, Bush is clearly someone who long ago made his way to that dark territory and back. Indeed, this is a quality in him that, whether they are conscious of it or not, serves to endear him to very large numbers of people. Rumsfeld, on the other hand, simply refuses to grant any force to whatever weaknesses may lurk to trouble him, and this, in a very different way, serves to endear him to a wide public as well.

These positive feelings about Rumsfeld are both affected and not affected by what is these days so ungrammatically called gender. That is, the traits his male and female admirers profess to admire in him are given very different names but point at bottom to be the same basic quality. Men are likely to say that they admire the way he knows his mind and talks tough and straight, or the way he manages so deftly to keep the press in its place, or, in more general terms, what he has done and is doing for the country. Women, on the other hand, tend to express their feelings about him less specifically, saying that they find him to be a particularly attractive combination of good-looking and smart and sexy. Both descriptions, however, can basically be summed up in a word that has for a considerable period of time been deprived of public legitimacy.

The word is *manliness.*

As it happens, before the administration of George W. Bush, the country had for eight years been governed by someone who was essentially a clever boy. Bill Clinton was undeniably intelligent, and under the right circumstances he could also be charming and ingratiating. But he was also weak and self-indulgent, somewhat uncouth, and still stuck on girls in the manner of an all-too-anxious adolescent. Many people claimed to appreciate and admire him, but most of them were little more than political partisans, his own people—most conspicuous among whom were liberal Democratic women. In the end, however, it turned out that what such women really admired and favored in Clinton was their own ability to keep his political feet to the fire. When he was caught out in a scandal born of his adolescent fevers, these women made a great show of their continuing support for him, which now rather nakedly revealed itself as merely a form of support for their own political agenda.

The point is that by the time he departed the White House there were few women and even fewer men who would with any sincerity have awarded Clinton the status of sex hero, let alone— O happy invention!—"studmuffin." That designation would have to await the arrival of a high-achieving, clear-headed, earnest, no-nonsense, Midwestern family man nearly seventy years old.

The times, in other words, they were a-changin'.

WHAT, THEN, was this change and what did it signify? Even after the flags were no longer flying from every rooftop, the leveling of the World Trade Center continued to leave a deep mark, probably deeper than they knew, on most Americans. Their country, after all, was no longer sitting in confident security between its two great oceans and its non-bellicose neighbors to the north and south, and there were people running around in it who were not merely criminal or crazy but trained and ready to kill themselves in order to help bring the whole place down. Along with its initial stirring of the patriotic juices this realization undoubtedly also gave rise to a new sobriety. As Dr. Johnson once so wisely said, the prospect of hanging concentrates the mind wonderfully.

Yet even so, it is doubtful that the events of 9/11—though enough to have sent the country into wars in Afghanistan and Iraq—would by themselves have been enough to account for the "discovery" of Donald Rumsfeld. Friends of his, particularly women friends, say that what has happened to him on this tour of duty is really nothing new, that people have always responded to Rumsfeld as they do now. But "people" are not the same thing as "the public." Nor could there have been anything in his past that would have reached as far into the popular culture as *People* magazine.

It was, of course, his regular and frequent appearances in the media, especially his two- or three-times weekly appearances at Pentagon press conferences, that did the most to gain him such widespread public attention. But that only raises the further question of why they went on watching. And even more important, what was it that they were seeing?

They began watching in the first place perhaps for no other reason than that their country was at war in Afghanistan. The Gulf War of 1991 had made not only the visual spectacle of high-tech warfare (or what seemed then to be the last word in high-tech warfare) but also the regular military briefings about such warfare a species of popular entertainment. But then, in the case of Afghanistan, though mopping-up operations went on, the war was for all intents and purposes over pretty quickly. Yet people continued to watch. They watched and got hooked on the by-now celebrated play between Rumsfeld and the Pentagon press, between Rumsfeld and his military cobriefers, between Rumsfeld and the people at the various military bases where he held town meetings, and between Rumsfeld and the television pundits who interviewed him.

Then with Operation Iraqi Freedom, a far more controversial war than the one in Afghanistan, Rumsfeld began to come in for a fair dose of press hostility. But by holding his ground and continuing to keep his critics at bay through the same manly traits that had won him so many admirers before, he managed to hold his own in the public approval ratings.

The consensus among many of Rumsfeld's friends is that the role he has come to play is somehow connected to his qualities and experiences as a wrestler. A champion wrestler, they explain, is someone who is always in condition for combat, who knows that he is solely responsible for the outcome of his battles, and whose victories—as his friend Ned Jannotta had remarked—are by their very nature winner-take-all.

There are undoubtedly parts of Rumsfeld's career to which such an idea about him would seem to apply. For instance, it would fit the White House chief of staff who was sufficiently confident of his moves to risk making enemies of some very powerful political figures, people, moreover, who had a few skillful moves of their own to make in return. It would also fit the CEO of Searle who not only sued and beat the Food and Drug Administration but who was twice prepared to jeopardize the sale of the company to Monsanto rather than give in to a pressure he was unwilling to accept. In both cases he certainly showed a special gift for going to the mat.

But the wrestler's gift, while it may play some unconscious part in what the public sees in him, does not by itself begin to answer the real question, which is, Why—after all those years in public life and in a job that is anything but glamorous—should he have become a popular hero? What is it about his particular brand of manliness that both men and women, viewing him through their inevitably separate lenses, find so steadily attractive?

In a discussion of Rumsfeld's ideas about how to make better use of the army—the ideas that have embroiled him in so much conflict—Victor Davis Hanson points toward the answer. Hanson believes that, as both a Princeton graduate and a former naval pilot, Rumsfeld is familiar with, but neither envious nor in awe of, the Eastern elite that dominates the American universities, government, and media. While in Hansen's view Rumsfeld is a great respecter of the intellectual richness of our best universities, he "nevertheless seems more at ease with the sounder practical judgment of Middle America. . . ."

His roots in the culture of Middle America do seem to account in very large part for the public's response to him. That culture, however, is not so simple a matter to characterize. To understand what it was (and is), one has to begin by looking back at the territory, namely, the prairie, that gave birth to it.

The prairie was a potentially rich but to begin with a hostile and unyielding terrain. The people who ventured to settle there from parts east needed grit and determination and, at least equally important, they needed to look after one another. And ultimately, once the soil yielded to the plow, what got planted there along with corn and wheat and soy was something that can only be called a culture of vitality. (Drive today through what used to be the prairie and you will see living, waving proof of what is meant when people refer to the United States as "the breadbasket of the world.")

Later, in the nascent city of Chicago, where the physical and social conditions at first seemed no less hostile to the idea of urbanity than had the prairie to the idea of fruitfulness, those Midwesterners once again did what was required in order to plant a truly vital community and watch it grow.[2] (Still later than that, in the suburban village of Winnetka, some of them managed to create a life that was to become a very special combination of comfort and striving, ease and great ambition, one that would keep large numbers of the children being raised in the community close to home and yet would send sparks of talent and enterprise flying downlake into the metropolis.)

Thus since its founding in 1837 as a village of some four thousand souls, and later as Carl Sandburg's "hog butcher for the world," Chicago has been imbued with a great faith in the possibility of enterprise. Even its notorious past as a center of Prohibition-era bootlegging and crime had about it an air of unflagging energy. Donald Rumsfeld's Chicago is, to be sure, very far from the old rough-and-tumble; it is a place of banking and manufacture and numerous pleasing civic amenities. In any case, what is perhaps most important about the city is that in both its identities—the early rough and the latterly benign and handsome—Chicago has been a community run by family men.

---

[2] A fascinating incident in Chicago's early history says something very telling about its ethos. As the city grew, it was discovered that the Chicago River, which ran through it from west to east and ultimately fed into Lake Michigan, was dumping human and industrial waste into that otherwise pristine body of water. Whereupon the city fathers brought in engineers who devised a system of pumps for reversing the flow of the river from east to west. How could such an undertaking and the spirit behind it fail to leave an indelible mark on the ethos of a community?

Now, a city run by family men is a city without a lot of airs, where status is distributed almost solely on the basis of achievement, and where lineage, if it doesn't exactly count for nothing, counts for much less than it does among the inhabitants of the country's two coasts. Such a city can be rather rough on those who are in one way or another either unable or disinclined to pull their own weight. At the same time, it makes for unfailingly good manners: Family men in the prairie-cum-Chicago sense are people who, in an option-ridden and self-scattering nation, continue to aspire to live and die among neighbors.

Washington, like New York, is a city not of neighbors but of colleagues. And nothing about Donald Rumsfeld seems more striking than the fact that for all the years he has spent there, he is not a Washingtonian. Rather he is very clearly the child of that prairie-driven culture of vitality. And he is also a Chicago-style family man. Life in America has certainly offered him a more than ordinary share of options, and he has without hesitation availed himself of them. Yet for all the various jobs he has held and the many places he has lived in, he is in some profound sense as deeply rooted where he started out as if he had never left home.

Furthermore, while Rumsfeld certainly takes a very hard-headed measure of the world and the people in it, there is not one drop of cynicism in him. After years spent learning the ropes in Washington and in business, he is as earnest about what he believes in as the boy who won that naval ROTC scholarship during his second year in college—perhaps even more earnest than that boy. Add to this the toughness to take on whatever he is convinced will serve his beliefs, whether it be a system of missile defense or the fashioning of a leaner and meaner and more easily dispatched American military for the twenty-first century, or even, should it be necessary, no more than the besting of hostile members of the press, and you have a very old-fashioned kind of American hero.

Which is exactly the point.

At some point in American popular culture the idea of "tough" came to be primarily associated with the connotations of "rough" and "ready to lash out." And at some point the idea of "manly" came to be associated with erotic artfulness rather than "household" and "family"—not to mention "country." These connotations and associations have been in force for a considerable time now. They matter deeply, as culture always matters deeply, because even people who have not consciously accepted them are inevitably influenced by the mood they generate.

That mood more than anything else expresses a wish to be cut free from burdensome responsibilities. The possibility of fulfilling such a wish sounds most appealing, particularly to the young, but the truth is, for a great number of Americans it has taken a whole lot of the fun and juice out of life.

"Something strange is happening to the American soldier," observes Victor Davis Hanson about Rumsfeld's army, "almost as if current popular culture were being married to nineteenth-century notions of heroism and sacrifice. . . ."

Well, that same something "strange" appears to be happening not only to the members of today's armed forces but to civilians all over America as well. There is, to be sure, no sign of any intention to return to the days of Queen Victoria—or even those of George and Jeanette Rumsfeld. Yet nothing, it seems, has come to lie so heavy on either the individual or the public chest as the ambition to lead an unburdened life.

Which by itself may explain the unshakable appeal of the man the public has taken to calling "Rummy": to manicured women and with-it girls, to successful men and dreamy-eyed boys, and to many liberal voters as well as conservative ones. For he exemplifies to perfection the vitality and the high humor that can be the rewards of a willingness, even an eagerness, to assume and embrace the burdens of responsibility instead of running away from them.

"Big Noise blew in from Winnetka," goes a jazz song of the 1940s, "Big Noise blew right out again." Unless George W. Bush is defeated in 2004, it is impossible to believe that Rumsfeld will be permitted to "blow out again" anytime soon. This means that he will proceed further with the transformation of the American military into a faster, more efficient, better integrated high-technology force. He did not, certainly, bring about this whole development all by himself; so large an undertaking required much help and participation and support. But it neither would nor could have happened without him.

And then there is his stardom, which has carried with it, and to some extent furthered, some kind of change in American attitudes. The popular "discovery" of Donald H. Rumsfeld spells the return of the ideal of the Middle American family man, with all that such an ideal entails in the way of vitality, determination, humor, seriousness, and abiding self-confidence, along with protectiveness toward loved ones, neighbors, and country. In the long run, this change may well be more important to the fortunes of his country than the changes he will have wrought in its armed forces.

It seems certain that the picture of Rumsfeld hanging on the dressing-room wall of my fashionable dinner companion during that warm New York evening will not be taken down from there anytime soon.